THE TRUTH WILL SET YOU FREE

TRUE TALES OF AN L.A. DEPUTY, 1959 TO 1988

BY ROB MEAD

ISBN: 979-8-9887138-3-8 (paperback)
ISBN: 979-8-9887138-4-5 (ebook)

Library of Congress Control Number: 023924428

Cover photo: *Lights from Palos Verdes Peninsula* (C.Miller)

Interviews, editing & project design: Linda Parker Hamilton

Thanks to John Kolman, author of *Rulers of the Night* for use of SWAT and SEG images.

Stories to Last
www.StoriestoLast.com
Oakland, CA

THE TRUTH WILL SET YOU FREE

TRUE TALES OF AN L.A. DEPUTY, 1959 TO 1988

BY ROB MEAD

Stories to Last Press

DEDICATION

FOR DONA, THE LOVE OF MY LIFE. She was the best thing on two legs. Looking at her was like watching the most beautiful sunset ever. And for my children and current and future law enforcement officers. It isn't always easy, but the truth will set you free.

TABLE OF CONTENTS

INTRODUCTION

Thirty Years in Law Enforcement

T HE MAIN REASON I APPLIED to the L.A. Sheriff's academy was because, as a nineteen-year old husband and father, I needed a job with a steady paycheck. As a kid, I never dreamed of becoming a cop. I never had a specific career goal, maybe because my mother's constant insults had snuffed out all my ambitions. Yet I spent three decades—from 1959 to 1988—serving as a deputy in the Los Angeles County Sheriff's Department.

Looking back, it all makes sense now, how I got there, and why it was a good career for me. I saw a lot and learned something new every day, and the work became a huge part of my identity. I worked with exceptional people whose dedication and humor I will never forget. Despite all the shit we saw, we had some great times, too. Most of my partners were great people who were special to me. I loved my job.

But policing can take a heavy toll. We faced trauma daily. Many of my colleagues and friends that didn't die in the line of duty died from cancer, heart attacks, drug and alcohol abuse, and suicide. Now, in my mid-80s, I'm one of the only guys left, one of the lucky ones who came out of the force fairly unscathed.

These sad statistics were part of the reality. We were taught to be suspiscious. We often faced death and sometimes, out of self-defense or the rule of law, we had to take someone down. No matter the context, taking a life can have lasting effects.

The job was disturbing and rewarding, frightening and inspiring. This book, my story, will try to explain why all these seeming contradictions are true. Hopefully, it will paint a clear picture of what it was like to be in law enforcement—patrolling, working the jails, special assignments on the SWAT team, and working undercover in L.A. during the decades of the 1960s through the 1980s as the county's population changed and grew, a time when drugs, gangs, and homicides were continually on the rise.

Despite all the bad experiences and the loss of people I love, I will always be grateful for what I have been able to accomplish as a deputy. I was able to help people, and that's what law enforcement was all about for me. The story of the retirement of Sergeant Billy Sands illustrates what I mean.

The Retirement of Sergeant Billy Sands

In 1980, I worked in the Organized Crime Division of the Los Angeles Detectives' Office. At the time, the Mafia, the Symbionese Liberation Army, and the Weather Underground were all considered big-time gangsters on the West Coast. We called them "OCs," the heavyweights of organized crime in L.A.

I got an invitation to a retirement dinner for Sergeant Billy Sands, my former partner and boss, a good guy. Billy came from humble beginnings in the South. He was also one hell of a deputy. He served twenty-seven years on the force and had worked as a background investigator on homicide, rape, and other criminal cases.

Billy and I often worked a beat together at the race tracks where many of the OCs hung out. We made our rounds at Santa Anita Race Track, Hollywood Park, and Del Mar Track in San Diego County. The OCs owned some of the horses, and there were all kinds of race fixing and criminal activity behind the scenes. It was a racket. At each race track, the Sheriff's Department had a reserved box. We'd go there in plain clothes, and, of course, we made a few bets on the horses to blend in. Billy loved to bet; we're all human. After the races, Billy and I would go to the jockey room to visit with the riders, observe, and maybe ask a few questions.

His retirement dinner was held at the Bonaventure Hotel in Downtown Los Angeles, a high-end place with a revolving restaurant and bar on the top floor. I sat with 200 other cops, the largest gathering I'd ever seen for one of these. The new acting sergeant and, surprisingly, the fire chief were at the speaker's table. The presence of the fire chief at a police retirement function was unusual.

The fire chief approached the microphone and said, "Billy, you responded to a rescue at the L.A. International Airport at Lennox Station. A baby, 18 months old, was choking and turning blue. You got there before the fire department and cleared her air passage. You remember that?"

Billy shook his head. He'd responded to thousands of calls in his career.

The chief continued, "Well, thanks to you, that baby started breathing again. She got her color back, and she lived. She's all grown up now, and she's here tonight." A lady in the audience stood up.

"She's now a nurse. Her husband is in the Navy. They have two kids. All of that is because of you."

There was not a dry eye in the place.

That Billy didn't even remember saving a baby's life was the point. Billy had helped that little girl because it was part of his job, and he had the right training to do it. He had saved lots of people.

Working in law enforcement meant taking care of people. People might think I'm crazy, but I wake up every day asking, what can I do for someone today? In my work and my personal life, I always tried to take care of others. Being in law enforcement for thirty years gave me that opportunity.

*East 1st Street,
Los Angeles,
1954*

CHAPTER 1

The Rookie, 1959

Growing Up in East L.A.

I GREW UP A TYPICAL lower-middle-class kid in East Los Angeles. It was a different neighborhood in the 1940s and early '50s than now. We had gangs, but they weren't like the gangs we see today with drive-by shootings and drug dealing. During those days, gangs were groups of disheveled youths waging territorial wars, fighting with each other, and occasionally stealing and vandalizing. In the late 1950s and 1960s, gangs like the Bloods, Crips, and Sureros—also known as the Mexican Mafia, despite having originated in the jails of Southern California, not Mexico—took over. They were regularly involved in strong-arm robberies, illegal dice games, burglaries, auto thefts, assaults, and drug sales.

In the 1940s, East L.A. was a relatively safe neighborhood where kids played in the streets. That included the time during World War II when the ethnic makeup of the neighborhood drastically changed. At the beginning of the twentieth century, East Los Angeles was a popular destination for Russian, Jewish, Japanese, and Mexican immigrants. Living east of the river and working in nearby factories or traveling by electric rail into Downtown Los Angeles, these families helped fuel the prosperity of the growing metropolis. With the onset of World War II, East Los Angeles became a predominantly Latino community due to an influx of Mexican workers who operated the machines in the area's burgeoning war industries.

Growing up in a multicultural community taught me that, no matter where they are from, families all want the same things: financial stability and a good life for their kids. That hasn't changed.

I was born in Chicago on April 1, 1938, an April Fool's baby, but grew up in East Los Angeles where my dad was transferred. He was a salesman for restaurant supplies, selling plates, utensils, pots and pans, bulk food, and the like. During World War II and until 1949, we lived near Boyle Heights in a place called Wyvernwood Garden Apartments at the corner of South Soto Street and East Olympic Boulevard. It was a huge complex. "Garden apartments" was an architectural movement in Southern California—planned apartment communities for middle-class people that typically offered each resident a patio or small yard. Later, garden apartments were reduced to shared green spaces to increase the number of units and income from tenants. There must have been a thousand of these apartments around us built cheaply to house returning soldiers and their families. Though my parents probably would've liked a house, we didn't have a choice. My dad didn't make enough money, and the housing market was impacted with no new construction during the war.

As a kid, a garden apartment was fine with me. There were lots of other kids around. One of my neighbors was a guy named Harvey Larson. He became a doctor and later delivered all three of my kids. He was an exceptional man, a great doctor, and a good friend. A pair of twin brothers lived around the corner from me and became good buddies. In the late 1940s, after the war, they had all this World War II memorabilia in their garage given to them by a relative. I was fascinated by the uniforms and the tall black boots worn by the "bad guys," the Nazis. The twins owned a German Luger, a Walther, and a real German helmet that even had a bullet hole in the temple. We played make-believe with all this stuff, and it gave me a lifelong interest in World War II history.

In my East L.A. grammar school, I excelled in math. And though some things about school weren't much different than they are today, some of the curriculum was different. I remember a demonstration they gave at school when I was in fifth grade to show the dangers of smoking. The demonstration involved a smoking machine and a live rabbit. The presenter put a cigarette in the machine, and we watched as the contraption smoked the cigarette down to the filter and collected the smoking residue in a clear tube. The man got a syringe, extracted the residue, and injected it into the rabbit. The rabbit died before us—one cigarette was enough to kill it. There is no way they could do anything like that today! But the demonstration worked on me because I've never smoked and have been a passionate anti-smoking advocate. I constantly told my smoker-patrol partners, "That shit will kill you." And it did. Most of them died of cancer.

One Positive Role Model, One Negative

My dad was a good man. He went to Howe Military High School in Howe, Indiana, where he received an award for being the most caring student on campus and was named Most Christian Student by his peers. The title meant that he displayed patience, kindness, self-control, and helped others. He was captain of the baseball, basketball, and football teams. His father had a successful furniture business in Chicago, but my father didn't want to work in the family business.

He was a great athlete and played a little semi-pro ball in the 3-I league: Indiana, Iowa, and Illinois. He even had a short stint with the Chicago White Sox, but he only was what the players called "a cup of coffee." He didn't stay long because he wasn't

13

good enough. Then, my father married my mother. It's significant to mention that they married before the Great Depression in 1929. My mother came from a lot of money. She grew up in a mansion on Longwood Avenue in the Greater Wilshire neighborhood not far from Beverly Hills. Her family employed maids and butlers, and she went to private school and the whole bit. Her father owned several banks in Chicago. He knew everybody, including Bill Thompson, then Mayor of Chicago, George Halas, who owned and ran the Chicago Bears, and even Al Capone. Marrying my mother presented my dad with opportunities he would not otherwise have had, but I don't know if that was why he married her.

Then, the Great Depression hit. Her father, my grandfather, lost all his banks, and my mother lost all her "royalty." She became a commoner, and, boy, was she bitter. She hated people. She would walk down the street, point, and say, "Look at that ugly person." She was mean to almost everyone, including me, my sister, and my father. She used to tell me and my sister, "I wish you were never born." She told my dad, "I should have married Joe instead of you. I should've never married you."

My dad wasn't happy in his marriage. How could he be? As we grew up, we could see the toll it was taking on him, even as kids. But we knew he cared about us. Other dads walked out on their families, but he didn't. He was an angel. He always took care of us.

When I was a kid, my sister asked my dad, "Why don't you leave Mom?" He simply said, "I can't let her raise you." He was afraid she'd turn us into monsters. Back then, fathers were not awarded custody. So, he stayed despite our mother's abuse.

My father was a settling force in our household, a true gentleman. Maybe that's why I always wanted to help people—to be more like him. He was a great role model and a huge influence. I knew I wanted to be nothing like my mother. She was my negative role model. I remember my sister went on a date once and returned late. My mother was mad. She screamed at my sister, hit her on the head with a frying pan, and split her head open. That was the kind of a woman my mother was. She was mean and vindictive, abusive, and always complaining. I don't like complaining and negative talk. It doesn't help anyone, especially the person doing all the complaining. And with her behavior, she had no friends. She and my dad fought all the time. It was so bad that I wanted to run away when I was five. I was talked out of it by my sister, who was seven years older than me.

In public, my mother's behavior always embarrassed me. When we went to a movie theater, if it was a musical, my mother would sing along out loud, completely oblivious to the other people around us. One time, when I was a kid, our family was at Knotts Berry Farm having dinner at the Chicken House, which was incidentally run by a friend of mine whose uncle, Wayne Collins, owned Knotts Berry Farm. Wayne Collins became my undercover name later on.

Playing football at California High School in Whittier, CA, 1955

When we were served our chicken, my mother looked at my plate and said, "How come his chicken is bigger than mine?" I was so embarrassed I wanted to hide under the table.

As a child, the values I learned from my father were fairness, compassion, and kindness. My dad's values kept me out of trouble. He was a good father, and I felt close to him, even though he wasn't always at home because he had to work and didn't want to be around my mother too much. I chose to be like my father and never act like my mother.

In my beloved Chevy hanging out after school with friends, 1954

My life has always had these kinds of contrasts, and I took these lessons from my childhood into my work in law enforcement. My goal was to treat everyone, even criminals, with respect, be considerate of others, and remain positive.

From Child to Man

Senior portrait, 1956

When I was in eighth grade, we moved from East L.A. to East Whittier into a brand-new, small house that my dad had worked hard to buy. There were vast new tracts of residential homes and apartment buildings in Whittier, which was once mostly agricultural land and oil fields and had become a new hub for commercial, industrial, medical, and institutional organizations.

16

It wasn't the house we were supposed to move into. My mother wanted her brother, a contractor, to build us a house in an upscale part of Whittier called Friendly Hills. But, like my mom, my uncle was a real jerk. He presented my dad with a bill much higher than anything they had ever talked about, much more than we could afford, and so we declined that house and bought the smaller one in a modest, middle-class neighborhood.

I went to work starting at age 13 as a box boy in a local market. I liked earning and was saving up for a car. I also started playing football about that time and was pretty good. I played throughout high school as a starter. In 1956, my senior year, I was scouted as a tight end by George Allen, the future Washington Redskins— now the Washington Commanders—head coach and Super Bowl champion. At eighteen, I was offered college football scholarships. One was to nearby Whittier College. It would've been easy. But I didn't take any of them. I was a lost kid with a crummy home life and didn't know what I was doing. Instead, I enrolled at the local junior college. Then, my girlfriend announced she was pregnant.

I was in love and so I married her and soon after, we had our first child. I was nineteen years old. We moved in with my in-laws into their small backyard casita. That was all the help they could give us. I grew up mostly dirt poor, and they weren't that well off either. It was tough, but I wasn't going to let my new family starve. I immediately quit school and went to work, securing two part-time jobs at local markets restocking shelves and one full-time job at Pacific Clay Pipe, putting plastic connector seals around pipes, an assembly line-type job.

It wasn't long before another child was on the way. We needed to get out of there and get our own place. The casita was tiny, and it was tense living with the in-laws. We started saving what little money we could. My wife was very attractive and made some good money by modeling, but it was part-time and infrequent. She got some other part-time work as a crossing guard. I had a collection of guns and started selling them one-by-one to buy food. I was pretty good with finances—that was the only good thing I learned from my mother—but our income was not enough to buy us a house. My biggest asset at that time was my car. I loved my car, a 1955 Chevy that I kept clean and polished, but I knew if I sold it, we'd have enough for a down payment, so I did.

That still wasn't enough. We needed a loan to complete the deal. The bank told me I couldn't get a loan unless I had a stable and secure full-time position, something career-oriented. I thought, *What the hell can I do?* I didn't have any particular skills. I thought teaching might be a good option, but I'd have to make time for college classes and student-teaching to get my teaching certificate on top of working full-time. I looked around to see what else was available to me. My wife's dad happened to be a highway patrolman. I had two neighbors who worked in the L.A. Sheriff's Department, one a lieutenant and one a captain. Talking to all of them, a career in law enforcement piqued my interest. I could do that.

I signed up to take the test to become a deputy sheriff in Whittier, where we lived. The test, a combination of physical and mental exercises in oral and written segments, was difficult. The written tests were especially hard, containing many math problems and "common sense" questions. You needed to get 70% of the answers right to pass. Luckily, I passed and was deputized on December 22, 1959, at the age of 21. Shortly after, we qualified for a mortgage and bought our house in Whittier for $13,000.

1960s Los Angeles

When I started my career at the end of 1959, more than six million people lived in Los Angeles County, nearly 35% of California's population. Los Angeles had grown like crazy in the previous decade, becoming a major urban center. In 1958, the Brooklyn Dodgers moved to Los Angeles, becoming the first Major League Baseball team west of Missouri, and in 1960, the Lakers basketball team arrived from Minneapolis. Los Angeles was on the map for more than filmmaking, although most people still considered it Tinsel Town, full of Hollywood movie stars, glitz, and glamour.

The Hollywood Walk of Fame opened in 1960 with a star dedicated to Joanne Woodward embedded in the sidewalk. The L.A. movie industry was well-established by then. In 1959, the University of Southern California, USC, offered the country's first undergraduate and graduate degrees in cinema and television, drawing even more dreamers to the area. That same year, Los Angeles-based toy company Mattel released the first Barbie, giving L.A. the reputation of beaches full of buxom blondes in

Program for the first Dodgers game on April 18, 1958. The Dodgers beat the San Francisco Giants 6-5 before a record crowd of 78,672.

Kennedy-Nixon presidential debate, 1960

19

bikinis. The Sunset Strip became a breeding ground for bands like The Byrds, Buffalo Springfield, Spirit, and the Doors. The Beach Boys formed not far away. It was also a place to see and be seen while cruising on Friday nights.

The world was changing all around us. Beatnik culture was turning into hippie culture: peace, love, and rock n' roll. Drug culture became more prevalent. Speed, psychedelics, and opioids were easy to buy on the streets. President Dwight D. Eisenhower signed the Civil Rights Act of 1960 into law. *To Kill a Mockingbird* by Harper Lee was published. After the first-ever televised U.S. Presidential debate between Kennedy and Nixon, Los Angeles hosted the Democratic Party national convention. When John F. Kennedy won the presidential election, there was a feeling of hope, especially among young people. But a shadow was cast over that hope because, that same year, the U.S. entered the Vietnam War, sending young men overseas to die and bringing protesters out onto the streets.

It started a tumultuous, experimental, power-to-the-people, culture-shocking, and redefining decade.

An Off-the-Streeter

I started work as an "off-the-streeter," meaning I was assigned on duty even though I hadn't been to the academy and had no military background. They gave me a badge and told me to suit up because, on New Year's Day, January 1, 1960, they needed as many warm bodies in uniform as they could get to man security at the Rose Bowl Parade. Also known as the Tournament of Roses Parade, it has happened annually on New Year's Day since 1890, with colorful floats adorned with tens of thousands of flowers, marching bands, and horse units parading down Colorado Boulevard in Pasadena.

"Suiting up" meant I had to buy all my equipment, which was standard practice at the time—uniform, shoes, belt, jacket, and gun. The top pay was $489 a month for a sheriff's deputy. It took a month's wages to pay for all the gear, which included a Colt Python revolver that cost ninety-three bucks. (Later, in 2019, I sold it for $3,500 to a policeman in Wisconsin.) It wasn't until 1962 that deputies no longer had to purchase their guns. By then, the Sheriff's Department issued uniforms and a Smith & Wesson Model 15 revolver. Every few years after that, we were given better guns to keep up with the firepower of the bad guys.

So, on January 1, 1960, about two weeks before I was due to start at the academy, I was in uniform at the parade in Pasadena. I didn't know anything. I'd fired guns before, but never a handgun. I didn't know how handcuffs worked. Maybe that's why I remember my first handcuffs' serial number to this day: Peerless Handcuffs 311032.

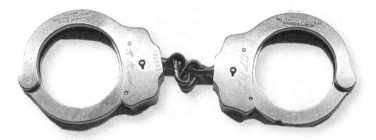

I was assigned to security for the Mounted Posse, a big thing at the time and a longstanding tradition. The Mounted Posse was a group of policemen on majestic and well-trained horses. My task was to guard the horses and the silver saddles on a side street while the Posse waited for their turn to march down the parade route.

Luckily, I worked with three experienced and exceptional deputies: Walt Lanier, Jules Streeter, and Fred Blewett, all proud Black Americans and good guys who remained friends all our lives. Honest to God, I saw little prejudice in my twenty-nine years on the force. Were there racial jokes and slurs among officers? All the time. Whether right or wrong, they were freely used in the 1960s through the 1980s. But in the department, they weren't used maliciously, and people were rarely offended. We took care of each other. I had partners that I'd die for. My partners came to my house socially, and I went to theirs. They were incredible people who were fun outside of work and took care of business on duty. Although we all came from different backgrounds, we all had the same job, and we did it better when we worked together.

Walt, Jules, and Fred guided me along, but they had their duties, so I was standing by myself in the street by the horses when this reserve deputy gestured and walked toward me. I knew him as a friend of the sheriff, a guy who had a lot of political influence and was a big political contributor.

The Mounted Posse in the Tournament of Roses, 1960

He said, "Deputy, see that white Chevy over there?" I saw the car parked about fifty yards away. He said, "Go arrest them for drunk."

"Yes, Sir," I said and started toward the car, but to myself, I thought, *Oh, God, what do I do?* I didn't have any sense of procedure. I approached the Chevy and looked in the driver's side window. Two guys were passed out inside. Immediately, I recognized the guy behind the steering wheel. He was a guy I went to high school with named Richard, who was a year behind me in school. Pasadena is about thirty miles from Whittier, where we lived as teenagers. I knocked on the window, waking him. Dazed, he sat up and rolled the window down.

"Richard," I said, "Get your ass out of here. A cop might arrest you."

His eyes got wide. But he heeded my warning and beat feet out of there. I didn't know anything about drunkenness in public or drunk drivers and the dangers. I was naive, and it was 1960. Luckily, they made it home without incident.

Richard always said he owed me for that. He cleaned up his act and eventually became captain of the Whittier Police Department. His partner became a lieutenant. Had they been hooked up by someone other than me, they could never have served in law enforcement.

Training at the Academy

I reported to the Los Angeles County Sheriff's Academy in mid-January and began my official training. It felt like being in the military. It was twelve weeks long, eight-plus hours a day, Monday through Friday, with a lot of physical work and situational training. It was stressful. But then again, law enforcement is stressful. We learned defensive tactics and how to do death notifications. We faced various life-and-death scenarios, making split-second decisions about whether to shoot suspects. We learned about using force, defensive driving, and pulling over and approaching suspects in cars. We were also taught community relations and how to treat people with respect. We learned about officer safety and, of course, how to write reports. There was constant physical training. We ran and lifted weights. They worked us hard. It was also taxing psychologically. Our superiors and trainers

A drill instructor shows how NOT to search a detained person at the Academy, 1960

always tried to say things that might upset us. To get cadets to crack and quit, they asked if our parents were married and if we were bastards. They had formal and informal inspections of our quarters, uniforms, and guns.

In the past, I had fired a lot of small caliber guns and B.B. guns as a kid in staged gunfights as we played. But at the academy, I became proficient with handguns. It wasn't just about aiming and firing our guns. We had to learn to care for them and keep them clean and operational.

Gun inspections were detailed. Most of us got in trouble because our guns were dirty and too oily, but not Jim. Jim was my age. I had known him as an acquaintance in eighth grade and never saw him again until we were both in the academy together. Jim always kept his guns perfect. He bought liquid mercury and ran it through the cylinder and the barrel. The mercury took out all the lead. You could buy it at the pharmacy then, but you had to be careful. If you heated the mercury, it could kill you, but I guess Jim knew how to handle it properly. He passed every gun inspection with flying colors, and some of the other cadets were jealous.

We had to memorize many codes along with the physical and scenario training. Dispatchers and deputies had to communicate in coded language in case criminals with scanners picked up our conversations. I learned a useful and interesting new vocabulary. We had a number for every model of car, listed alphabetically. For instance, an Audi was a 1, and a Chevy was a 6. Most of the deputies drove Chevys in the 1960s. We had numbers representing different types of people, too. An example of a code might be, "The 70—meaning a male—is in a 6 (a Chevy) with a 69—that's his wife—and he's got a 71—that's a kid. He's north on the major—meaning he's northbound on the freeway." That would allow our guys to jam him at an intersection, surround him, and pull their guns if necessary. The goal was always to arrest suspects without shots fired or undue force. That was always the goal, but it didn't always work out that way. We learned to try our best to de-escalate situations using our wits and sometimes even humor.

One day as part of our training, we rode along in an official vehicle to learn patrol and arrest procedures. Two officers sat in the front seat, while I sat in the back with another trainee who was a bodybuilder, a huge guy. Patrol cars are specially modified so that a suspect can't open the doors from inside the rear seat. There was a fight somewhere, and we answered the call to break it up and make an arrest if necessary. When our patrol car pulled up to the fight, the other trainee tried to get out of the back seat and join his fellow officers. He was so pumped up on adrenaline he couldn't think straight. He couldn't figure out why the doors weren't opening. He was going crazy, banging on the windows, trying to push open the doors, and bouncing off the sides.

Seeing this, one of the deputies told the suspects, "If you guys don't stop fighting, we're going to let King Kong out of the back seat, and he's going to take care of business. Stop the fight." That's all it took to defuse the situation, and when they got back in the vehicle, we all started laughing.

The academy was tough, but I made it through and learned a lot of useful skills and knowledge. I felt like I got all the training I needed to start working a beat. I turned twenty-two before I completed the academy in April of 1960.

I earned my badge!

25

CHAPTER 2

Working the Jails, 1960 to 1963

AFTER GRADUATION FROM THE ACADEMY, I was assigned to work for the Corrections Department at the Los Angeles County Jail. All rookies at the time needed to work as a guard before going out on street patrol unless we had prior police experience. It was part of our training as officers. Working in the jail gave us the opportunity to learn how to deal with people of all kinds. Jail was the perfect place for this, and it was a real eye-opener for a 21-year-old like me.

I reported for work at the Hall of Justice at 211 W. Temple Street in the Civic Center district of Downtown Los Angeles. The county jail was inside the Hall of Justice Building on the 10th to the 14th floor. Some inmates had been there for a few days, others for years. It depended on their court dates and how long their trials were. The cell blocks were built for 1,800 inmates but housed 4,400. Overcrowding was a huge problem that led to a lot of tension. Four inmates were in each cell with beds, and three more inmates slept on mattresses the floor. In addition, we had what we called "the freeway," a barred and locked hallway that ran the length of the cells, which was around 20. Guys slept on mattresses on the floor in the freeway as well. Each morning, they had to roll

Hall of Justice

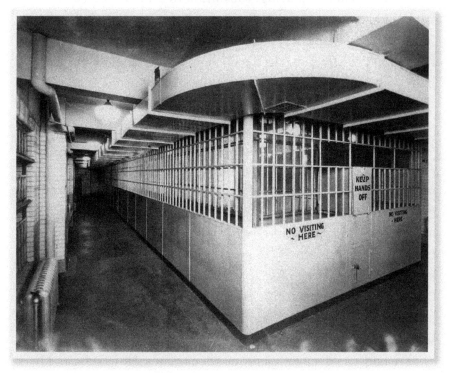

Visiting Area in the Hall of Justice

up their mattresses and stash them so we could use the walkway. That made for tight quarters and a lot of people to manage. There was also gang and racial tension, so it was always best to be alert.

All new inmates were sprayed for lice. We had trusties with spray guns full of chemicals helping us. A "trusty" was an inmate with no prior criminal record who had been sentenced to a "bullet," a year or less in prison. By working in the jailhouse, they could reduce their time to as little as eight months and ten days if they maintained good behavior, worked jobs in jail, and stayed out of trouble. They wore brown jumpsuits instead of the blue ones the other inmates wore. Trusties weren't the most honorable people in the world, but they tried their best. I told them, "Look, you screwed up and got caught. I'll cut you some slack. If you do well, I'll give you extra visitation days and take days off your sentence. We take care of each other."

Some still failed, making deals with other inmates, stealing food, and getting into fights. But most of them kept their heads down and did the tasks assigned to them, working in the laundry, helping to prepare meals in the kitchen, scrubbing floors in the bathrooms, or assisting the nurses in medical. The good ones would even tip us off about inmates planning to hurt one another or taking meals from others. It always helped to have a snitch, but they had to be careful.

One trusty helped with the delousing. The inmates were instructed to get naked, and the trusty sprayed them with chemicals everywhere on their bodies. It didn't matter if someone was arrested on a drunk and disorderly and was only spending the night or they were headed to prison for arson or assault: they got sprayed. The guys even had to bend over and spread their butt cheeks. That must have hurt. Though I never saw it, I heard that some guys were so filthy that the lice jumped off them when they were sprayed down.

We had one doctor to serve all the inmates. He was busy. The inmates called him the "witch doctor." He'd examine people who complained they were sick and give them Tylenol or prescribe other mild medications. In jail, prisoners could see a dentist, but he didn't fill teeth, he pulled them out. Officers would line up maybe twenty people complaining of a toothache in the dentist's office. A trusty followed the dentist down the line, holding a tray with twenty syringes of Novocain. The dentist gave the first inmate a shot, then the next, then the next, all the way down the line, until they had finished all twenty. By the time he had given all the shots, the first guy's mouth was numb, so the dentist would take him in and pull his tooth out. Then he'd do the same with the second guy, and so on.

Might Makes Right

When the other new cadets and I first started working in the jail, we were briefed by a superior officer. He said, "Okay, there's dos and don'ts. First of all, do not take any letters from prisoners to deliver to wives or see any family members of any prisoners on your own because you can get compromised. The inmate might say, 'Hey, Officer, can you take this letter? When I go to the joint, it won't get there. Can you take it and deliver it to my wife?' Don't do it."

We were always told: Beware the three B's: bills, broads, and booze. They would get you in trouble. We also had the expression: "Don't shit where you eat." Occasionally, a deputy wouldn't take heed. It never worked out well for him. One deputy who didn't follow the rules met this gal, a prisoner's wife, and they started having an affair. He got caught and fired.

I spent two and a half years working in the county jail and met all kinds of men, from gangsters and murderers to guys in for petty theft and bar fights. Some good guys in there had unfortunately made some bad choices. There were some evil men, too, who operated on one particular value: Might Makes Right. It was a different life behind bars.

The jail had specific cell blocks for different types of inmates. There was a section for snitches, one for inmates on Death Row and another for Mafia guys and members of other gangs. They had one cell block, High Power, located on the tenth floor, next to the attorney's room. High Power was reserved for juveniles who were being tried as adults.

There were three types of inmates in the jail that we referred to as "green-lighted," meaning that other inmates might try to harm or murder them—snitches, child molesters, and ex-cops. The people who were the most hated were the snitches. The inmates called them *ratas*, Spanish for rats. The other inmates would kill snitches if they got their hands on them, so we had to keep them safe. One of our jobs was to escort groups of inmates to the showers once a week. Every time we took the snitches to the showers, we had to lock the other inmates in their cell blocks. The other inmates yelled insults and threats as the snitches walked by. If they had been out of their cells when the snitches walked by, an inmate might have stabbed a snitch, going for his carotid artery. The weapon of choice was a toothbrush heated at one end so a Gillette blade would adhere to the melted plastic and harden. Might Makes Right. That was their thing.

I worked primarily on the 11th floor in four cell blocks containing probably five hundred inmates. Among other things, I was in charge of feeding all 500 guys. A trusty helped me serve the meals. Two days in a row, the meal cart was missing food—a loaf of bread or something. On the third day, I turned around and saw an arm go into the cart. The trusty had been stealing food.

"Roll up your gear," I told him.

A cell block across the hall had four Black Muslims as inmates. We had a good relationship because I treated them respectfully, and they acknowledged and appreciated that. I treated everyone with respect. Some guys weren't smart enough to figure it out, but these men were. The leader of the group, Cox, was smart. He had been arrested on federal drug charges and would leave soon for McNeil

Island Federal Prison in the Puget Sound area of Washington State.

I said, "Mr. Cox, I've got a thief here. I'll take care of you—I'll give you extra food and extra visits for you and your three compadres—if you guys take in another roommate. I never want to have a problem with this guy again."

"Sure, Mr. Mead. No problem," said Cox. "So, here's the deal: while he rooms with you, he never gets a bunk. He sleeps on the floor."

Cox said, "I got you."

And that was it. That's how we took care of situations in the jail. These inmates weren't going to hurt the thief. I knew that. It was enough punishment for the culprit to be in a cell with guys he didn't know and to sleep on the floor for a while. He never stole food again.

It was important never to demean anyone in jail and never take their manliness away. I called inmates Mr. Jones, Mr. Collins, or Mr. Cox to show respect. As I saw it, a large part of my job was to make things as nice as possible for each inmate, given their situation. Or, using an expression they often said in jail, "Don't piss backwards on me." I expected mutual respect. The trusty-turned-thief screwed up and got caught, so there had to be consequences. Otherwise, I'd undermine my authority, which would be unfair to everyone else who hadn't been stealing.

Conversely, if an inmate behaved decently, I could get him a 12:01 release. That means if he wanted to get out of jail on a certain day, I could let him out at 12:01 a.m. He'd go home one minute after midnight on the appointed day. But if he was a jerk, I'd write a memo recommending keeping him in jail until 11:58 at night, resulting in another full day in jail.

My attitude was: I won't cause you any problems, so don't cause me any problems. The majority of the inmates understood that. Most of them were okay, and we got along.

Meeting the Devil

While the majority of the guys in the county jail were in for doing something stupid, fueled by want, a disconnect to consequences, or drugs, I also met some truly evil humans. Doyle Terry was one of them. He had dark, menacing eyes, looked like the Antichrist, and had no morals. In 1960, he pulled a bank robbery in Long Beach and got away with it until he and his accomplice pulled over on the side of the road on Seaside Boulevard in the area of the Terminal Island Naval Station, five miles from the robbery. They were trying to ditch the accomplice's car and were pulling the battery out of the Cadillac before taking off again in Terry's Chrysler when a patrol car rolled up next to them. Back then, we didn't have the kind of police communications that we have now. Individual officers didn't get R.O.V.E.R.S. (Remote Out-of-vehicle Emergency Radios, two-watt, 8-channel, hand-held radios) until the early '80s. In the 1960s, handheld radios were difficult to produce and too costly to give to each officer, especially in large cities like Los Angeles, so all we had was the radio in our squad cars.

So, there was Terry with all this stolen money in the back of his truck and a revolver underneath his sweater. A nice young policeman named Officer Owings and his partner saw these guys with two cars, one with the hood up. Officer Owings was probably thinking, *Hey, this guy is in trouble. Maybe I can help him with his car.* But Terry was thinking, *This cop is going to arrest me.* So, he shot the policeman right in the head then turned the gun on Owings's partner, hitting him in the leg and continuing to shoot until he ran out of bullets. Owings had not even taken his gun out of the holster. Terry and his accomplice took off in the Chrysler, running over Owing's body.

During his trial, Terry claimed that shooting the officers was an accident and denied committing any robberies. His lawyer was a screwball named Frank Duncan. I've got a story about him, too.

Terry was convicted of robbery and first-degree murder. It turned out he had committed a slew of robberies. Before that, he had been charged with child molestation and furnishing narcotics to a minor. He had absolutely zero conscience. I steered well clear of him. He would kill you as soon as look at you, and I didn't need that.

Then there was Don Catchall. He got booked about the same time I started working in the jail. We had gone to high school together. Even then, he was a loser, always up to no good. He ran a robbery at a market in Monterey Park, adjacent to East Los Angeles. A young policeman saw what was happening and went after him. Don made it to the getaway car, but unbeknownst to the cop, another suspect was in the driver's seat. He saw the policeman coming up and shot him down. The policeman was wounded but alive. Don got out of the car, saw the policeman writhing in pain on the ground, pulled out his gun, and shot him dead. He got caught and sent to prison. I saw Don often in jail but never spoke to him. Thinking about him as the kid I knew in high school was strange. But he was also a cop killer, so we had nothing to say to each other.

At one point, I was working on the C decks, which had six floors and six tanks. There was one guy behind bars named Billy Monk who later died in the gas chamber for his terrible crimes. He killed people, raped, and tortured them. Terrible stuff. While he was in the county jail awaiting trial, he got hold of a Gillette razor blade, put it in his mouth, and swallowed it. He made sure I was watching. I was standing only about four feet away, on the other side of the bars, when he did it. I immediately called the hospital.

"Stupid ate a razor blade," I told them.

"Send that fool up here!" they said.

When they brought him back to his cell in one piece a half hour or so later, I called the hospital and asked, "What did you do?"

33

"We gave him a cotton sandwich: two pieces of bread with cotton in the middle and made him eat it." I guess the cotton wrapped around the razor blade, and he passed it.

Why did he eat a razor blade in front of me? I don't know. Maybe he thought I'd testify in court that he was crazy, reducing his sentence, but that never happened. Some guys in prison were truly insane. Others were "crazy like a fox," pretending insanity to reduce their sentence or get sent to the psychiatric hospital. As anyone in the judicial system can tell you, the psych hospital is much worse than jail, but I guess it's better than the electric chair or the gas chamber. We'd probably say today that Billy was sociopathic or psychopathic. In the 1960s, a lot of mental illness went undiagnosed.

Whatever the cause of his actions, Billy Monk went to death row and didn't stay there long. He was executed for kidnapping on November 21, 1960, at the age of 26, one of the last people in the U.S. to be executed for a crime other than murder.

The Rubber Room at Lincoln Heights Jail

Then there were those inmates who were temporarily crazy, going bonkers because of withdrawals or reactions to the drugs they took just before joining us in Justice Hall. We had a padded cell for inmates who were out of control called the Rubber Room. Nowadays, they're called Safety Rooms, or De-escalation Rooms, or Cool-Down Rooms, or Seclusion Rooms, Violent Rooms, or Padded Cell Systems. The materials have changed, but they're still typically equipped with floor and wall padding and impact-absorbing floor tiles and other safety features.

A Cool-Down Room today

Inmates who get violent need a place to stay to keep themselves, their fellow inmates, and correctional facility staff safe. In our day, that was the Rubber Room.

Sometimes, the cops would arrest a guy but couldn't tell if he was truly crazy or acting crazy because he was drunk or high. So, they'd bring him to the jail and leave him with us to dry out. We'd put him in the Rubber Room. If the inmate continued acting crazy, we'd take him to see a shrink because we weren't doctors or experts in mental illness. The court would decide if the man should be committed to a psychiatric hospital.

Or he'd go into the Hot Rod Tank. That was for the guys who were moving out-of-control and screaming. They were all revved up. The tank contained bunk beds with porcelain toilets on the floor. One inmate dove head-first straight into the toilet, cracked his head open, and broke the toilet.

This one guy was waiting for his court date and acting out of control, so we put him in the Rubber Room, and he took his feces and spread it all over the walls of the cell. To get him out, three cops and I got a big mattress and held it in front of us while another officer opened the cell door. We pushed him up against the wall and handcuffed him. We had to hose down the entire cell after that.

35

No Hope with Dope

A lot of people in the jail were drug addicts. I've seen drugs ruin lives. In 1960, the use of amphetamines, marijuana, and heroin was on the rise. Cocaine didn't come into vogue until the 1970s. I saw a lot of that, but when I started in the sheriff's office, heroin addicts were the most abundant.

I remember an inmate telling me that being an addict was like starving. He said, "The only thing you want to do is get high. I don't care where I put that needle. If you're starving, you don't want to cook the food. You want to eat it. If I want to get high, I want to get high right now."

Addicts who use heroin leave behind track marks on their arms due to carbon. They put the heroin in a spoon and heat it, then suck it up into a syringe and, in so doing, include carbon from the match, which creates black track marks where they shoot up. That's why many heroin users will tattoo the area to cover up the tracks. I even heard of guys that had a $1,000-a-day drug habit. They were stealing all kinds of stuff to support their habit. Some men turned their wives into prostitutes. The addiction took over. Drugs were the most important thing in their lives. They didn't care about anything else, not about their families or their kids. They just wanted to get loaded. I always say: *There's no hope with dope.*

Late in 1962, after a few years at the Hall of Justice jail, I was transferred to the Biscailuz jail, a medium-security unit off Eastern Avenue in East L.A., a satellite jail to take care of overcrowding in the main jail. It was named for retired Sheriff Eugene Biscailuz, who organized the California Highway Patrol and served 26 years as the 27th Sheriff of Los Angeles County. It was a fenced unit for about 600 inmates.

While there, in 1963, a new sergeant came on duty at the jail. He'd left Dope, meaning he had been an undercover officer in Narcotics. He was one of the arresting officers—along with a young deputy named Sherman Block, who later became the county sheriff—who arrested comedian Lenny Bruce on narcotics charges while in a Los Angeles taxi cab. Lenny Bruce was what we called a "Hype," a heroin addict who used a hypodermic needle to shoot up. At the time, the comedian was home on recess from his trial in Chicago for public obscenities.

The new sergeant and I used to work the PM shift together, from 4 p.m. to midnight or longer. He was a nice guy, and we had some interesting conversations. The only odd thing was that he always wore sunglasses, even at night. I thought that was strange until the reason became clear a few months later when he was fired. He was on heroin, which screws your pupils down to pinpoints, and he didn't want anyone to see.

Being a dope cop is dangerous. Drug dealers are paranoid and always have guns because they think they might get robbed or attacked. Life is a constant war to them. So, in dealing with them, you've got to talk, look, and sound convincing. You can't talk like a cop. You can't say "vehicle." You can't say "suspect." You can't carry a department-issued gun. The bad guys hate two kinds of people the most: undercover cops and snitches. They kill anyone if they find out a person is either one. When it came to snitches, they didn't even torture them because they thought torture was too good for them. Once, during a court case, an inexperienced judge said to an arresting officer, "You better give up your snitch, or you are going to jail." That was unusual. The officer knew what would happen to the snitch, but it was an order. He outed his snitch. That judge was stupid. Two days later, the snitch was found dead. The criminals had injected battery acid into his veins. You find incompetent, ignorant, thoughtless, or corrupt judges here and there among the good ones. At least, that was true in my day.

The story was that the sergeant had become an addict on the job. He was on an undercover assignment trying to buy drugs. The dealer looked at him sideways and said, "We think you're the Man. Prove you're not. You'd better shoot up or we're going to kill you." He didn't have many choices in that situation. If he was going to get this guy for dealing and not get killed, he had to prove he wasn't a cop. He took the heroin and ended up getting hooked. Heroin is incredibly addictive. When someone regularly uses heroin, they usually develop a tolerance, meaning they need larger and more frequent doses of the drug to get the desired effect. The way the sergeant described it, it wasn't his fault that he became addicted, but he just couldn't shake it.

Just before he joined me at the jail, one of his drug cases was reopened, and the sergeant had access to the drug locker. His superiors checked the locker and found all the heroin gone. It had been swapped out with lactose powder or milk sugar, which looked like heroin. They started checking around and realized the sergeant had taken it and was actively using it. The case against the drug dealer was kicked out without the evidence, and the sergeant was fired. It was sad. He seemed like a decent guy if it weren't for the drugs. I don't know what happened to him after he was fired.

Doped Horses

Many crimes were perpetrated by people taking drugs and still are, but while at Biscailuz, I also learned about crimes involving people giving drugs to racehorses, a common practice at the time. From the 1930s to the 1950s, horse racing had been one of the most popular sports in America, a sport of the rich and famous. Tracks were where Hollywood stars went to be seen, and they often owned horses. But by the 1960s when I was a cop, the rest of America had caught racetrack fever, and race tracks in Southern California were frequented by hustlers trying to rip people off. Racing could be a dirty sport.

Because of my relationship with the inmates, they used to tell me stuff. One day, I was doing my rounds when this inmate went snitch and slipped me some juicy info. He told me which horse owners at the local track were doping the horses with cocaine for claiming races. In a claiming race, the horses are sold at the end of the race. So, horse owners could take a weak horse, dope it up with coke to make it perform better during the race, and then sell it for more money than it was worth. By the time the coke wore off, the horse was already in the buyer's stable, and the sucker would realize he spent all his money on a horse that couldn't run. If the drugged horse won or placed in the race before it was bought, those winnings also went to the seller, adding to his profit on a doped-up nag.

I didn't know anything about horse racing at the time except for what I saw on TV, but this was too important to keep to myself. So, I wrote a memo to Vice telling them about the doped-up horses. I never heard back about it. I'll never know whether or not they caught anybody, but when I patrolled the tracks myself in the 1970s, this knowledge was useful. As far as I know, doping racehorses might still be an issue today.

Another Thug

Yeah, I met some real characters at the Los Angeles County Jail. One day, LAPD brought this gangster-thug into the jail—6'2" and between 230 and 240 pounds, all muscle. He was an animal. Two good-sized officers accompanied him. While we processed him, we put the guy in what we called the "holding cage," a large, screened-in area with thick wire mesh. After we secured him, he hit the screen door and said to me menacingly, "I want you." I thought, *Oh shit!*

One of the sergeants, Kermit Kynelle, saw what was happening and said, "Deputy, let me book him." Kermit was also a big guy— 6'2" and about 215 pounds. He was a good dude too, and smart. He won a lot of money as a contestant on *The $64,000 Question*, a quiz show on TV. I gestured for him to take over.

When it came time to book the gangster, Kermit grabbed a deputy from the Identification Room, where the officer was photographing and fingerprinting people. His name was Curtis

39

Howard. He came in with a towel over his shoulder to wipe the ink off his fingers from the booking process. He always had that towel hanging over his shoulder. I knew Curtis for a long time after that. He was an outstanding deputy and a good guy.

During the booking, Curtis stood on one side of the suspect, Kermit on the other. Suddenly, the assailant hit Kermit in the face, leaving a gash down his cheek, below his eye. That was a big mistake. Curtis and Kermit subdued the thug and showed him the "error of his ways." I didn't see any more after that. The incident left a scar on Kermit's face, though.

Sadly, Kermit later committed suicide. There was a lot of suicide among law enforcement—after everything they saw and experienced, some became depressed, and some never recovered from the PTSD.

Walking Gangster Mickey Cohen

"Walk Mickey Cohen." Those were my orders from the Brass.

I had a good reputation. I was always on time. I never sniveled or complained. I was good with the inmates, so I think that's why they assigned me to escort the infamous West Coast Mafia leader through the new inmate process.

Mickey Cohen was unusual from the start. For one, he was short, 5'5," and Jewish, while most Mafia guys in those days were Italian or Mexican.

40

Mickey started as a professional boxer, then became muscle for the Mafia. When Mickey became an enforcer for the Chicago Mob, killing and maiming anyone who got in the way of their profits, he gained a reputation for violent tendencies and irresistible charm. Rumors of this made their way to Bugsy Siegel, another Jewish mobster. Soon, Mickey was killing for him, too, while helping to set up the Flamingo Hotel in Las Vegas and managing the hotel's sports gambling operations.

Then Mickey turned celebrity mob boss and took over L.A. He schmoozed with famous entertainers like Frank Sinatra, Sammy Davis Jr., Dean Martin, and Jerry Lewis. Legend has it he used to sign autographs on the streets of Hollywood. His fame and tight hold over the Los Angeles crime scene landed him the nickname "The King of Los Angeles." An action-thriller movie called *Gangster Squad* was 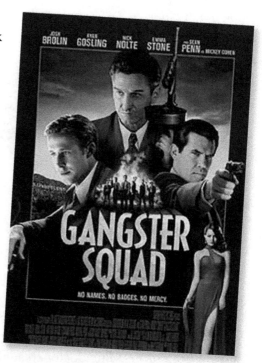 made about how the LAPD "waged war" on him and his gang. The film, starring Ryan Gosling, Nick Nolte, Emma Stone, and Sean Penn, was based on a non-fiction book of the same title by Paul Lieberman. Mickey is also featured in the book and movie *L.A. Confidential* by James Ellroy.

The day I booked Mickey, he was dressed to the nines in alligator shoes and a matching belt. He could carry off that look. He didn't give me any trouble as I walked him through. The real gangsters generally didn't. It was the chumps that gave me trouble.

Mickey Cohen was no chump. He was a made man and the biggest mobster of his time. He was deeply violent, a trait that had helped him rise through the ranks, but you would never know that from how he appeared and acted when I booked him. Maybe he was looking for sympathy, but Mickey was cordial and did exactly what he was asked to do. He played the elderly gentleman, a harmless-looking guy. To a 22-year-old newbie, he seemed grandfatherly. He was only 48 years old, but my youth and his hard living made him look much older.

Once processed and escorted to his VIP cell, I also walked Mickey to the hospital. He had a medical court order because he suffered from ulcers. The doctor treated Mickey by giving him Maalox, which wasn't much of a treatment really.

I always had to be on guard when walking him. It wasn't just that he was a high-level criminal that made him a VIP. He had a lot enemies in the jail who would like to beat the crap out of him or kill him if they had the chance.

I knew that Mickey lived by the Mafia code of "I scratch your back, you scratch mine." But two seasoned deputies about five years ahead of me fell prey to this code. Part of Mickey's criminal activities was running bets and fixing races. He controlled the national horse racing wire service, and could fix any race he wanted. While in the jail, he told these deputies which horse to bet on at Santa Anita, the race track outside Los Angeles. He promised they'd win big. They placed their bets and, like Mickey said, they each won a ton of money. When they told Mickey of their "good fortune," he told them, "Okay, now you gotta do me a favor. I don't want jail food. I want you to bring me salami and cheese, the good stuff. Smuggle it in for me. I did you a favor. You owe me now." The deputies felt they couldn't refuse, probably thinking, "You don't say no to the Mob!" So, they sneaked the food in for Mickey, got caught, and got fired.

But fixing horse races was nothing compared to Mickey's other activities. He built a crime syndicate that included narcotics. He controlled the labor unions. He had a prostitution ring and even worked over movie studios by demanding a cut from the studio executives. When he started to schmooze with Hollywood's finest, he hired private tutors to teach him etiquette so he could fit in. He was smart and crafty, but, as the saying goes: "power and money corrupt." He was amoral and had no respect for human life. Mickey was not shy about killing anyone or admitting that he had. "I have killed no man that in the first place didn't deserve killing by the standards of our way of life," he said in a live interview.

But you know how they got him? Do you know what I was booking him for? Tax evasion. Mickey had murdered, tortured, extorted, and was even involved in the publicized blackmail of Lana Turner, whose lover, John Stompanato, a made Mafia enforcer, was killed in her bedroom. Still, we only ever got him on tax evasion—twice. When I met Mickey, it was his second time in jail, and it was in between his first arrest and his second that he had become an international celebrity.

Along with his crime racket, he ran floral shops, paint stores, nightclubs, casinos, gas stations, and a men's haberdashery. He was rumored to have operated an ice cream van on San Vicente Boulevard in the Brentwood section of Los Angeles. He was even mentioned in *Time* magazine.

43

After awaiting trial in the county jail, Mickey Cohen was sent to Alcatraz, where he became the only prisoner ever to get bailed out from the island prison. When he lost all his appeals, he was taken into custody again and sent to the Atlanta Federal Penitentiary. An inmate there went after Mickey with a lead pipe in an attempted assassination. Mickey survived that incident.

When he was released in 1972, he spoke out against prison abuse. The ulcer he had been diagnosed with turned out to be stomach cancer. He underwent surgery and then toured the United States, making television appearances, still enjoying his infamy. He died in 1976 of complications from a second surgery.

The Murderess & Her Boy

The jail wasn't the only place I saw strange characters. There were some even in the courtroom. One of the strangest and most off-putting of them was a defense attorney named Frank Duncan. He was not a good lawyer; he was known to be arrogant and humorless. I testified in court several times when he was defending a suspect. He was a short, little man with owl-shaped eyes, a pompadour haircut, and an obvious lisp. There were rumors he used to give his clients drugs in court. But worse than that was what people said about him and his mother, who happened to be on death row in 1962.

Everyone knew his mama. They called her Ma Duncan. Some people whispered that Frank and his mother had been boinking each other before she went to prison. I don't know how true that was, but without a doubt, Frank was a mama's boy, and they had a strange relationship. When he was 29, he shared an apartment with his mother, Elizabeth Ann Duncan. She would follow him to his court cases, cheer when he won, and lash out at the district attorney when Frank lost. She had been in over ten marriages, sometimes getting married to a new husband before divorcing the previous one. No one knew how many children she had, although when she was on trial for operating a brothel in San Francisco and passing bad checks, she admitted in court that she had four kids, but Frank was her favorite.

One day, fed up with his mother's clinginess, Frank moved out of her house. He lived on his own for a short while but moved back in with her after his fifteen-year-old sister died unexpectedly of a spontaneous cerebral hemorrhage. Ma Duncan would not hear any more of his talk of moving out again. She threatened Frank, cried, and cursed at him. When he still wouldn't listen, she attempted suicide with an overdose of sleeping pills. Frank rushed her to Santa Barbara Cottage Hospital. At the hospital, he met a nurse named Olga. She was pretty and sweet and took good care of Ma Duncan. Before long, Frank had fallen in love with Olga and they started dating.

Ma Duncan would have none of it. She would not share her son with another woman. She told Frank to dump Olga. She even threatened the girl with harm if he didn't, but he wouldn't listen. When Olga announced to Ma Duncan that she and Frank were going to be married, Ma replied, "You'll never marry my son. I'll kill you first." She repeated this to Olga's apartment manager. Frank and Olga continued dating. When Olga got pregnant in 1958, they secretly married.

Ma Duncan found out. She was so enraged that she considered kidnapping Frank. She said, "I wanted to talk some sense into him." To keep the peace, Frank bounced between his apartment with Olga and his mother's house. Rumor has it he checked into a Santa Barbara motel with Olga on his wedding night and hurried home by 1:30 a.m. so his mother would see him there in the morning. After that, he spent evenings with Olga but almost always slept at his mother's. Even that was not enough for Ma Duncan. She started calling Olga and harassing her over the phone. She went to her apartment and screamed threats at her. Olga was so terrified that she moved apartments twice, but each time, Ma Duncan found her by tailing Frank when he went to visit his wife.

Olga told Frank about Ma Duncan's harassment, but evidently, he didn't believe her or was in denial.

Eventually, Ma Duncan decided on a more permanent way to end things between Olga and Frank. In 1958, she hired two Mexican farm laborers from Oxnard, California, to kill Olga. She promised to pay them $6,000. The men lured Olga out of her apartment one night by telling her that Frank was in the car drunk and asking for her. When she looked into their car, they pushed her into the back seat and beat her with the butt of a gun until it broke. Then they drove her into the mountains in Ojai, strangled her, and buried her in a shallow grave in a culvert that ran under the road. She may still have been alive when she was buried.

Friends started to look for Olga. By that time, Frank had been spending so much time with his mother that he hadn't been to see his wife for ten days. The police took a special interest in Ma Duncan when they found out that she had hired an ex-convict to pose as Frank while she posed as Olga and succeeded in getting a Ventura County judge to annul her son's marriage.

The police arrested the two guys on an unrelated charge. Fearing they would give her up, Ma Duncan told Frank the men were blackmailing her. To protect his mother, Frank went to the county jail to get the two men into more trouble for blackmailing his mother. Upon hearing this, the men confessed, giving up Ma Duncan to the police. They even took the cops to the unmarked grave where Olga was buried. They were probably also angry because she had only paid them $360 of the $6,000 she had promised.

Ma Duncan was convicted of first-degree murder. She called the whole thing a "frame-up to hurt her Frank." Frank hid in a Hollywood apartment rented under an assumed name until the cops tracked him down. Nonetheless, he represented his mother in court and proclaimed her innocence. She pleaded not guilty by reason of insanity. When asked on the stand why she did it, she said, "I didn't want to lose Frankie. I couldn't stand life alone, and I knew it."

Frank defended his mother to no avail. Ma Duncan was sentenced to death for killing her daughter-in-law while the young woman was pregnant with Ma's unborn grandchild. Even on the day of her execution, Frank was in court trying to get her execution delayed while she was being led to the gas chamber at San Quentin State Prison. On August 8, 1962, she became the last of

"Ma" Elizabeth Duncan's mugshot

only four women to be executed in California, right after Barbara "Bloody Babs" Graham, who allegedly suffocated a woman in a botched robbery attempt. Ma Duncan and her accomplices were also the last triple execution in the state. Her last words were, "I am innocent. Where's Frank?"

It appeared that Frank was more grief-stricken over his mother's arrest and sentencing than his wife's gruesome death. I heard he barely showed an ounce of grief for Olga. After it all happened, he relocated to L.A. County to practice law, which is where I ran into him in the courts. I heard he married a female lawyer, divorced again, and tried to stay out of the headlines. He was a strange guy.

The Coroner and Marilyn Monroe

After about a year at the Hall of Justice, the booking office expanded and moved to the ground floor. I often had to wait there for arriving prisoners. The coroner's office happened to be around the side of the building from where I waited, just through a car tunnel. One day as I stood there, the coroner came out of the door dressed in his white lab coat and holding a bucket in one hand labeled "brains" on the side. I kid you not. That caught my interest, and we started talking. He introduced himself as the deputy coroner, Thomas Noguchi. He told me, among other things, that he had performed the autopsy on Marilyn Monroe, who had recently passed away on August 4, 1962, in her Brentwood home of a probable suicide, a barbiturate overdose.

"It was a terrible sight," he said. He want on to describe her as unkempt, with dirt under her fingernails, her hair frizzy and short, the brown roots showing. She had purple blotches on her face, and her neck was swollen from having died face down. I found that interesting and sad. I didn't follow celebrities much and hadn't heard how desperate and depressed she supposedly was at the end. Of course, that part of her story is all over the internet now. But when the coroner described what he saw, the news was fresh. The public was still in shock, mourning the 36-year-old star. What a tragic situation. What a loss of a beautiful person. You never know.

FINAL 5¢ **New York Mirror**

Marilyn
Monroe
Kills Self

Found Nude in Bed...Hand On Phone...Took 40 Pills

STORIES ON PAGES 2, 3. PHOTOS ON PAGES 2, 3 AND CENTER FOLD

Begin Her Life Story — Page 3

Like any workplace, we had plenty of gossip. While I was doing the court run to West Los Angeles, I became acquainted with a county marshal, a handsome guy. One time, I caught him leaving the courthouse with an expression of mild excitement. I asked him what was going on. He told me he had to serve papers at a famous singer's house, a crooner (I won't say his name). I saw him again a few days later and asked how it went. He said simply that the crooner's wife was nice. Two months later, the singer divorced his wife for adultery. Although I never knew for sure, I always wondered, did the marshal have an affair with her?

I had to report one day to the Beverley Hills courthouse as a police witness in a drunk driving case. Prior to its renovation in 1982, the old courthouse was beautiful, with high ceilings and dark, ornate rosewood walls. I sat and waited for the hearing of the suspect I arrested. I waited, and I waited some more. There were good, decent judges, and then there were guys like this judge, who I'll call S.G., who used the bench to play God. While everyone in the courthouse looked on, this judge sat on the bench talking to a prostitute, a curvy woman with long legs wearing little more than a napkin of a dress. The judge's eyes sparkled a little as he listened, and he occasionally smiled at something she said. This went on for 45 minutes.

Finally, Judge S.G. addressed the court, "We have six drunk driving cases today. Due to the complexity of the court calendar, I'll see three randomly selected. The rest are excused."

That day, a few DUIs got off, not because of justice, but because of luck, because the judge was enjoying flirting with a woman and may have arranged an afternoon tryst with her. Who knows if those drunk drivers who were let off the hook learned their lesson or did it again, maybe hurting somebody next time?

An Inside Scoop on the Liston-Clay Fights

While I was working in the attorney room in the jail, I made fast friends with the boxer Art Aragon, also known as the Golden Boy. Of Mexican descent, he grew up in East Los Angles like me. Art had been a high-contending lightweight boxer from 1944 until 1960, amassing a career record of 90 wins (61 by knockout), 20 losses, and 6 draws. In retirement he had gone into bail bonds. That put him in the attorney room fairly often. A colorful guy, in the 1950s through the 1970s, he acted in movies too, sometimes playing himself and, being good-looking and charismatic, was popular among the Hollywood crowd, even romantically linked to Jayne Mansfield and Marilyn Monroe. He was also great friends with Audie Murphy, one of the most decorated soldiers in World War II turned Western actor and songwriter, someone I greatly admired.

Art Aragon

In February 1964, boxing's heavyweight world champion Sonny Liston lost to a new boxer, an 8-1 underdog named Cassius Clay, who the world would come to know as Muhammad Ali. Liston gave up the fight at the opening of the seventh round. In a rematch that May, Ali won with a first-round

50

knockout. It's now known as one of the greatest sports moments of the twentieth century. And one of the most controversial.

Soon after the second fight, Art told me he heard from the light heavyweight champion, Archie Moore that the first Liston-Clay fight was very questionable. He didn't say "fixed," just that the promoters at that time were looking to clean up the fight game. Liston was a gangster and ex-con. At 20 years old, he had been leading a gang of thugs committing muggings and armed robberies when the St. Louis police caught him. They called him the "Yellow Shirt Bandit" for the color shirt he wore. But being in the penitentiary might've been the best thing that ever happened to Liston. It's where he learned to box, and by 1962, he was the world heavyweight champion.

But even as champion, he was associated with racketeers, possible heavy drinking, and he went back to prison for a short stint for assaulting a police officer. To top it off, the mob owned his boxing contract. Fight promoters were not happy about his affiliations or reputation.

In contrast, Mohammed Ali was a fresh face. He had won the 1960 Olympics. He had no baggage. He hadn't yet revealed his faith and his membership in the Nation of Islam (which he did shortly after taking the title from Liston). The powers in the boxing hierarchy wanted him to win the fight, and he did. Ali was a great boxer, no question. But was Liston paid off to guarantee the win? Or because the odds against Clay paid out to the mobsters? Were the cuts under Liston's eyes and his shoulder injury enough to keep him on the stool or exaggerated for the loss? We'll never know, but even those on the inside, like my friend Art, were suspicious.

In 1970, Sonny Liston died of a supposed heroin overdose in Las Vegas. Even that was controversial. Those close to him said that Sonny hated needles and avoided them even at the doctor's office. That led to the speculation that it was murder. Yet another unsolved mystery.

CHAPTER 3

Bus Driver of the Convicted, 1963

I N 1963, I WAS TRANSFERRED to transportation. I worked with other deputies to deliver inmates by bus to the courts for trials and back again to the jails and to look after them while they were in transport. The inmates had to be tried in specific courts, depending upon where they committed their crimes and what their lawyers worked out. We moved prisoners from the jails in Malibu, Santa Monica, San Pedro, Long Beach, Industry, Alhambra, Pasadena, and out in the San Fernando Valley, Van Nuys, all over the county. We took them to court as far west as Santa Catalina Island and north to Lancaster, near Palmdale and Kern County. Catalina is about 100 miles from Lancaster with a channel to cross. That commute made for a long day.

On any given day, there might be 2,000 inmates going to court, with each bus containing twenty of them. We had an entire system to move them safely and humanely. For one thing, they needed food and water. Before we took off, we made lunches for everyone. We prepared boxes filled with sandwiches, fruit, milk, and chips, one for every prisoner on each bus. At lunchtime, we handed them out while en route. Not all the prisoners liked the lunches we made. They thought they were in a rolling restaurant, I guess. You can't please everybody.

LASD Crown bus and prison guards, late 1950s

At the jails, we showed paperwork to the deputies and told them who we needed to escort that day and to where. The inmates would be escorted out in four-man chains, cuffed, and loaded onto the buses. These were big Crown buses painted black and white with bars over the windows. A metal wall separated the passengers from the driver's seat so they couldn't see or attack the driver.

When returning them to prison after their court hearings, we had to identify the prisoners housed in each jail. I would say to my partner, "Hey Collins, give me your last three booking numbers." He would look at the list for that particular jail, say Malibu, and reply with something like, "Six, Four, Two." That's how we referred to the prisoners, by their booking numbers. We'd gather the three inmates and deliver them to holding cells until guards could escort them back to their regular cell blocks.

Transporting female inmates along with male inmates was tricky. We reserved one area on the buses for the women because the male prisoners always tried to say things to the females, and not things of the highest quality, as you can imagine. We had to arrange the seating as best we could so the men wouldn't bother the women.

We also had special transportation for gang members, snitches, and celebrities. We couldn't put the snitches in the group buses for the same reason we couldn't house them with the general population in jail: in case they got killed. Not only would that be ugly, but it might also mean the loss of a witness, and the snitch's family might sue the department. Two officers were assigned to take special prisoners to court in such situations. O. J. Simpson was one such special prisoner in 1994. Death row inmates were also special cases, as were pregnant women, and inmates diagnosed with tuberculosis.

I once got tuberculosis from a prisoner during transportation. I didn't know the prisoner was ill, but I felt sick soon after and got an immediate headache. A doctor gave me a pill, and I was told I contracted T.B. After the next pill, I felt woozy, but with the medicine, I recovered. A good friend who worked homicide also caught tuberculosis on the job. When we met up, he said, "It pisses me off! I can't drink for a year!" That part didn't matter much to me. I was never much of a drinker. More important to me was disclosure of each inmate's condition, which would allow me to protect myself and others.

After a few months of working in transportation as a supporting officer, my superiors thought I should drive the bus. Driving a vehicle of that size sounded terrifying! I reported to the L.A. Riverbed, where a trainer instructed me while I drove one of the big Crown buses down the wide, concrete surface of the dry bed. I had to learn to turn, brake, signal, and work the doors.

My first trip as a bus driver for the Sheriff's Department was with a fellow sheriff's deputy named Herb Loverling, a good friend. Both of us were new drivers. We had to pick up a group of Catholic school kids and nuns and take them on a field trip to show them a police heliport. The drive up to the helipad was on a narrow road. I was white-knuckling the entire time. The last thing I needed was to get into an accident and hurt nuns and children! Thankfully, we made it there and back unscathed. It's interesting that they tested our bus driving on innocent civilians. I'd like to think they just had confidence in us. But it could have been a sink or swim lesson.

I drove a lot after that. We did frequent pick-ups at the drunk tank out at Old Newhall Jail near Magic Mountain. They had a setup specifically for drunks. We called these guys "grapes." Once, I drove an empty bus there to pick up a bunch of grapes to take back to the county jail where their release would be processed since they had served their time. We loaded up about twenty-five prisoners. I received orders to stop at Van Nuys Court on the way to pick up other prisoners that were done for the day, as well as their paperwork.

The bus driver is like the captain of a ship. Even with other deputies aboard, I was the one that made the final decisions. When we arrived at Van Nuys, the other deputies—there were usually two besides the driver—went in to get the prisoners and their files.

One inmate on the bus yelled, "Hey, I've got to go to the bathroom."

I felt for the guy, but with the other deputies occupied, procedure meant he had to hold it. "I can't let you guys out," I told him from the driver's seat, "We'll be here for five minutes, and then we'll be back in the county jail in ten minutes, fifteen minutes tops."

No sooner had I exited the driver's seat and stepped to the ground outside when I heard a splash. The inmate had urinated in his shoe and poured it out the window. I shook my head. There was never any telling what someone was going to do next. A shoe urinal? It was unreal, but I guess when you gotta go...

The buses rode higher than regular cars, so the prisoners always checked out the "talent" in the cars that passed. That's what they called the ladies. Occasionally, we'd drive past a car in which a woman was giving a guy oral sex while he was driving. Of course, that drove the prisoners crazy. Most of them were young men who had been in jail for three months or a lot longer and hadn't had any action.

Some of the prisoners we transported were dangerous and high escape risks. I transported many guys like that. Some of them could pick a handcuff with a paperclip, and I remember watching a training demonstration that showed it was possible. Luckily, handcuffs have changed since then, but it was a real worry in the 1960s, so usually we moved these inmates in the back of squad cars.

One time, I escorted a high-risk prisoner to the Van Nuys Airport. The Modesto Police Department had arranged to fly down in a small twin-engine plane to pick this guy up and take him to the courthouse in Modesto. I was the only officer there waiting with him, but he didn't give me any problems. The plane arrived, and I handed him over. It was a PSA airplane, Pacific Southwest Airlines, which we used to call Perform Sexual Acts, an example of the crass humor that was part of the job's daily culture. I stayed to say hello and chat with a few of the stewardesses. They seemed to like cops. I was married then, but it was not a happy marriage. My wife and I had been trying to give it a go for several years, but I was pretty sure she had "other interests." In a way, I couldn't blame her. We married so young. Other than our children, we didn't have much in common. It was clear that we weren't in love with each other. Like my dad, I felt more and more like I was staying in it for the kids. So, it was nice to flirt a little. I was still just 25 years old.

Then one day, it became more than flirting.

Playing with Fire

Though there weren't many in the department, we had some excellent female deputies. One of them was assigned to work with me in transportation. This woman was beautiful. She had platinum blonde hair, looked like Jayne Mansfield, and drove a '63 Stingray. She turned heads everywhere she went and drove the inmates nuts. Everybody was chasing that skirt. But it became clear very quickly that she favored me.

We were bringing a bunch of inmates back to the county jail from Inglewood Court one day, and I could see her glancing at me repeatedly. Our duty completed, we started chatting. She was married but very unhappy in her marriage, she told me. Then she came on to me. I didn't want to cheat as a married man. But I was angry, lonely, and susceptible. And this beautiful woman who wanted me felt the same.

There was one major issue with getting involved with her. Her husband was a fellow cop. Not only a cop, he was big in the Sheriff's Department, both in respect and stature. Everybody loved him. He was a get-it-done kind of guy, upstanding, a good cop. And I knew he'd probably kill me for sleeping with his wife. But as the saying goes: "A hard cock has no conscience." The woman and I started sleeping around. She liked me even more once we started our affair. I treated her with respect and care. And I showed her the value of oral sex. Her husband had never provided her pleasure, ever. Now, that's a crime.

We saw each other on and off for two and a half years.

Then, in one moment, the affair came to a sudden end. One evening, her husband tailed us back to our rendezvous spot, a motel. He sped to a stop in front of us, jumped out of his car, and pointed a .45 at me. That scared the shit out of me! His wife said something to calm him down and left with her husband, both of them squabbling as they drove away.

That was it for me. It woke me up. She wanted to continue the affair—even after that. She said she wanted to marry me. But I thought of my dad and his sense of honor, of his staying with my witch-of-a-mother to care for my sister and me. I told her no. The adultery wasn't good for my soul, and I wanted to take care of my kids. I wanted to do the right thing, even if it meant being unhappy. I never screwed around again during that marriage. I saw the error of my ways.

Not long after, the woman deputy tried to kill herself with an overdose, but thankfully failed. She and her husband parted ways. She somehow injured her back, left the force, and retired on disability, moving on to a security job at Lockheed-Martin or Douglas Aircraft, one of those two. Out of curiosity, I looked her up years later. She had moved to Arizona and was dating a doctor. I hope she was happy. She was three years older than me and has since passed away. Her ex-husband, the model deputy, died prematurely of lymphatic cancer.

As for me, I tried to make my marriage work, but six months later, my wife and I divorced. In the meantime, I finally started doing patrol duty.

CHAPTER 4

Patrolling the Streets in Norwalk
1964-1966

IN 1964, I WAS TRANSFERRED TO the Norwalk Sheriff Station. I couldn't wait to finally go out on patrol. My first partner was also my training officer, Charlie Ellis, a street-smart and stand-up guy. Charlie and I were assigned car 44 and started out working the night shift. On one of our first nights, we got a call to go to Transcon Trucking Company in Pico Rivera. Pico Rivera and Santa Fe Springs were contract areas for the Sheriff's Department in Norwalk. Rather than having separate police departments for each of these relatively small towns, with all the communication systems and personnel, it was cheaper to contract for services. It was the same setup in other towns in the county. They also relied on our homicide unit to respond to calls in their area.

Transcon shipped goods to department stores like Saks Fifth Avenue, Bullocks, and May Company. The manager told us, "Man, we're getting slammed. We've lost $400,000 worth of goods in the last two months. It's gotta be an inside job." He said half the coats and half the watches in the warehouse were gone. "My insurance is killing me!"

Charlie thought about it and came up with an idea. "Here's how to handle it," he told the manager. "At the time clock where people punch in, put a locked box and tell your employees that any information from anyone regarding the recent thefts will earn the person and his or her spouse a two-week vacation in Hawaii."

He got a name in two days. Charlie solved that problem quickly and non-violently by using some common sense. I admired him; he was a real straight shooter. He became a good friend.

In 1964, we were issued breathalyzers for the first time. Any gadgets developed before then to measure blood alcohol content— one was called the Drunkometer— weren't reliable. So, the breathalyzer was a big

1960s Breathalyzer

breakthrough for law enforcement and road safety. We could test blood alcohol levels noninvasively and quantitatively, and very quickly determine if someone was too drunk to drive. In 1964, people were considered too drunk to drive at a 0.10 blood alcohol level instead of the 0.08 level of today. Sometimes, we pulled over drunk drivers so far gone that when we opened their car door, the driver fell out.

One night, we pulled over a guy and gave him a breathalyzer test, which he promptly failed, but he had a good attitude and didn't give us any problems, so I drove him home in the squad car while my partner followed in the guy's car. On the way, the man told me he was in the middle of a divorce. Since it looked like I was heading for divorce, I could feel for him. We put his car in his garage, gave the keys to a neighbor, and put the guy to bed. After that act of kindness, we had a friend for life in him, and he became a snitch for us.

We took care of people, and that feels good. That's what it was all about for me. Of course, people require different kinds of care, depending on the situation and their attitude. It's vital to pay attention, listen, be observant, and get as much information as possible to make a sound decision. I have to say though that the majority of the time that I decided not to take someone to jail and let them face natural consequences instead resulted in positive outcomes. Overall, I've always found the old expression true: You get more with sugar than with vinegar.

Deputy Humor

It helped to add a little sugar to our patrol job too, since the stuff we saw on a daily basis could be so bleak. Pranks were common in the department, and my partner Charlie loved to play pranks. Sometimes, we arrived on a scene as first responders, and sometimes we were backup for car 45, who were on the same beat. We thought the guys in car 45 were a little too fat, dumb, and happy, so a prank was often in order.

This one time, we assisted them in breaking up a fight, and no more officers were needed to get the situation under control, so we radioed in, "Code 4, no further assistance," and left the scene while they wrapped things up. Charlie was a smoker. Before leaving the scene, he took out a cigarette, poked a hole in it, and stuffed a firecracker inside. Then he lit the cigarette and placed it under the seat in car 45. The cigarette had to burn down to light the fuse, giving us ample time to wave good-bye and be off. Five minutes later while driving in their squad car: *BAM!* They thought they had been shot. Then they realized they'd been pranked. It drove them crazy.

We used to use teletype machines in the office for reports and communications. The machines created all these little paper dots as they punched holes in the paper, like a three-hole puncher. Charlie would gather the dots, put them in the vents of the other car, and open all the vents. When the guys started the car, the paper dots would fly all over the interior like confetti. It looked like the Macy's Day Parade inside a patrol car. The other guys appreciated a good prank and used to play jokes on us, too.

Some of the guys were funny without even trying. One night I reported to Norwalk to work the graveyard shift and was stashing my stuff in my locker room with Charlie, and another officer beside us had his locker open. Inside it, I saw a large calendar with a date prominently circled in red.

I asked, "Is that your birthday or your anniversary?"

"No," he said. "The girl at the donut shop is going to be eighteen that day."

I finally finished training for patrol with Charlie and was assigned to the day shift with a new partner. Charlie and I remained friends, though. Ironically, it was those cigarettes that got him in the end. I told him, "You should stop smoking." A few years later, while working vice, he died of lung cancer.

Trains Rucker

Along with pranks, the deputies loved handing out nicknames to each other. One of my favorites was "Trains" Rucker. There were many freight train lines through the Norfolk area and a lot of railroad traffic. One day, the railroad crossing arm broke and until it was fixed, a deputy named Rucker was assigned to direct traffic and keep cars back when a train was coming. It was a long and boring shift.

At one point, a lady rolled up in her car just as Rucker was stopping traffic for a train coming through. Out her window, she pleaded with Rucker, "I have to get to work. Please will you let me through? I'll be quick."

Rucker decided there was enough time before the train arrived, so he told her to go ahead. And wouldn't you know; her car stalled on the tracks. What are the chances? And she couldn't get it started again, probably was in a panic. Rucker tried to push the car, but the train was getting closer and closer. Finally, he pulled her out of the driver's seat to safety, and the train hit the car and destroyed it. When we heard about that at the station, Rucker never had another name. We called him "Trains" forever after.

Missed Bullet

We all make our mistakes. You just learn from them and hope the consequences of your error aren't too bad. One of my mistakes was losing a convicted criminal.

As I started one shift, the jailer at Norwalk, George Ames, a good friend who became a captain before retiring, told me, "We've got a guy in custody. He's in here for rape and he's hurt his hand. We think he hit it against the wall, and that caused the swelling. We don't know if it's broken or not. Take him to Studebaker Hospital."

The hospital was just shy of two miles from the station. I took him inside in handcuffs, naturally. The doctor asked me, "Officer, would you remove the cuffs? I want to check his wrists." As soon as I did, I got a call from George, checking on the prisoner. While I was taking the call, the guy beat feet out the door. I chased after him into an open field, repeatedly yelling for him to stop, but he kept running. I fired a shot that missed him, and he disappeared. I called for backup, but we couldn't find him. Luckily, they caught him a few days later before he hurt anybody else.

As for the shot I fired, I believe I'm lucky that I missed. In 1964, we were trained and encouraged to shoot a fleeing felon rather than allow them to escape. The law today forbids law enforcement from shooting unless your life is in danger, such as if the suspect turns around with a gun pointed at you or if some other imminent danger is present. But in 1964, cooperation was key, and running could cost you your life.

Back at the station, my colleagues reinforced this. While writing my report, a lieutenant named Wally Hunt, a smart guy but without much on-the-ground experience said to me, "You know, Bob, if you had shot him, the county would have covered you."

The other lieutenant on duty, Paul "Stubby" Strohman, once a semi-pro football player who later became a good friend, said "Bob, the only thing you did wrong was miss that motherfucker." Incidentally, we called him Stubby because he had lost part of a finger and was a short, stocky guy.

Shortly after, when I was working in Norwalk and still living in the casita behind my in-laws' house, a neighbor told me he had a friend in Wyoming with a ranch on 80 square miles of land where we could hunt called Campbell Ranch. He said we could see 300 antelope in one day. On a long weekend, I drove up there with my brother-in-law, who was a fellow deputy.

I was generally a good shot, and on our first day of hunting, I shot an antelope right in the head. I walked over to the animal lying still on the ground and stared at it. It was a beautiful creature. Gutting it made me gag.

That was the last time I ever shot an animal. That innocent creature didn't do anything to deserve getting shot. At the time I thought it seemed easier to shoot a criminal than that antelope. Later I came to realize that neither would have been easy on me. I'm one of the lucky ones that never killed anyone while on duty. It does something to most men, taking a life, even if the person shot is a criminal.

The Corvette in Pico Rivera

One of the things I learned while patrolling was to spot the unusual and check it out. Profiling is not racial profiling if you're really on the ball. It's responding to an element or behavior way out of the norm for any particular community. Sometimes the investigation would amount to nothing, but most of the time, it led to criminal activity.

I was patrolling one night in a high-crime area of Pico Rivera where there were a lot of drugs. All the cars on the road were beater cars, the usual in that neighborhood. Then, my partner and I spotted this Corvette parked on the side of the road. It even had a custom paint job. It didn't match the area. We got the license number, but before we could check it out, we got a call for a shooting at a topless bar three miles away. We put on the sirens and headed over. Other cops were already on the scene, an arrest was made, and peace was restored without any problem. We circled back through the neighborhood, but the Corvette was gone.

About ten days later, we saw the same car. We immediately received a call from dispatch of another emergency three miles away: a robbery with a possible kidnapping. We beat feet down there. Once again, deputies were already on the scene. We were backup and not needed. We drove back to finish checking out the Corvette, and once again, it was gone.

About four days after that, I was working overtime on a day shift when I spotted the same Corvette at a Shell gas station on Rosemead Boulevard. This time the driver was present, along with a blonde woman in the passenger seat. I asked them both to get out of the car and ran the driver's name. He was an ex-felon, recently released from Folsom Prison. His record and suspicious behavior made it pretty clear to me that he had somehow been involved in the recent crimes in Pico Rivera.

I told him, "I know where you live now. If you ever do that again, I will torture and kill you."

That particular wave of crimes stopped.

Given all the controversy about law enforcement in the 2020s, these words may seem severe, but I learned in the county jail that you had to talk to criminals in a way they understand and took seriously. If I had said, "Sir, please don't do that again because it upset us," that guy, living by his own rules, wouldn't have stopped his criminal behavior. He might've thought, *Oh yeah? I will do it again and see what this cop does.* No, I had to tell him how it was going to be in a way that would sink in. Most of the time, these guys had never learned or experienced the language of courtesy. They looked at that as weakness, not kindness. Had the guy been cooperative or obviously law-abiding, it would've been a different story.

My job was to protect the community and law-abiding citizens. Crime can have far-reaching consequences, so I didn't worry about talking tough with unruly suspects. And I only used physical force when absolutely necessary. It would've been inappropriate in that situation.

Another tough talk situation that really stands out took place when I was on patrol in South L.A. in 1966. I apprehended an O.G. and after cuffing him, this guy narrowed his eyes at me and said, "I'm going to kill you."

I looked back at him and said, "Okay, you get one shot. And if you miss, I'm going to kill you. Then I'm going to rip your head off and defecate in the hole."

He didn't give me any more backtalk. In order to be effective and not make mistakes, you had to learn to address people according to their behavior and character. I never had a problem with anyone: inmates, suspects, colleagues, supervisors, victims, witnesses, snitches, none of them. But it took that kind of awareness and flexibility.

As a matter of fact, it seemed to me that rewards work as well as consequences to encourage desirable behavior. I saw it work with my kids. While at Norfolk, I went to the brass with what I thought was a good idea. I told them, "Let's use the coffee fund to buy some gift certificates from McDonalds, the donut shop, or wherever to hand out as awards to good drivers." The coffee fund was a collection put together by the deputies and staff, so it would cost the department nothing. If we saw someone helping a stranded driver, being a good defensive driver, or waiting for a pedestrian, we could reward them. The brass dismissed the idea. I don't know why. It was a shame; it made sense to me. Maybe the supervisor thought I was crazy or couldn't be bothered to change things up. I still think it would be a good idea.

The Kid with a Starter Pistol

I learned that people can get into a lot of trouble when they're just not thinking. We were working an overtime shift and driving near El Rancho High School in Pico Rivera when suddenly, we heard a loud *BANG!* The sound came from the apartments across from the school. We called for backup and ran into the building. We didn't know if someone was getting shot or what.

We found three kids. One of them had a starter pistol like the kind used at track meets that fires blanks and makes a big a sound and flash. The kid holding the gun hesitated and then put it down, his eyes wide. "I was thinking of pointing the gun at you and firing it," he said, "It's only a starter pistol."

I said, "Young man, I see a flash, I hear a bang, I think you're trying to kill us. I'd have gotten my shotgun and blown you out of your shoes. I'd have dusted you. You would have been history." That got his attention.

"You don't do that," I said. You don't do stupid things like that, got it?"

The kid nodded nervously. I could only hope he learned from the incident to think through his actions more carefully.

A Super Cop

It didn't happen often, but on a couple occasions I ran across fellow cop who could use the same lesson. Once I was assigned an academy trainee while doing my rounds, and we happened to get a burglary call.

"Okay," I told him, "You're my second. Let's go." When we arrived on the scene, the door to the house was open. "You go around one corner, I'll go around the other, and we'll call for backup," I told him.

When the backup arrived, I met the deputies out front. "Where's your partner?" they asked.

Where was my partner? It turned out that he had gone inside, even though I told him not to. I wrote him up. He could've gotten us all killed. He thought he was a super cop. He was already what we called "badge heavy." That's how we described guys who come out of the academy mean and ready to kick ass. Instead, he got kicked off the force. You can make certain mistakes as a cop, but not the kind that can get you or your partner killed. Over the course of my thirty years, I was never injured or had a partner injured on the job. That was important to me.

Irish Jerry Quarry & the Cue Stick

I saw plenty of injured people though. One evening, we got a call about a fight at a bar across from the station called the Neutral Corner. The Quarry family owned it, Jerry Quarry and his brother Mike, both young professional boxers. Jerry debuted as a heavyweight in 1965 at the age of twenty and had a popular following. The press called him "Irish Jerry Quarry" or "The Bellflower Bomber," or "The Great White Hope," a nickname indicative of the lingering racism of the time and one that Jerry took issue with.

A drunk patron in the bar had walked out with a pool cue. Jerry followed the guy out to get it back. The patron, a big man, six-foot-six and around 300 pounds, smashed the pool cue over Quarry's head, opening it wide. Jerry wasn't about to let that go unchallenged. Even though he was only 190 pounds and six feet

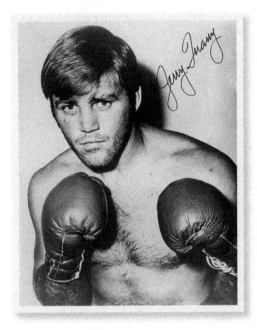

tall, he was tough and well-trained, with a mean left hook.

According to the deputy on the scene, Jerry destroyed the other guy. He broke his jaw and his nose with a single punch. Because he didn't start the fight, there were no charges against Jerry. But he had to postpone his next fight—with Muhammad Ali—while his cracked head mended. It required thirteen stitches.

The moral of the story is: Don't hit a professional boxer over the head with a pool cue!

Unhappy Endings

It was always satisfying to stop crime, but we didn't always see happy endings. I was working out of the Norwalk station when my partner and I responded to a call about a burglary. A television had been stolen from a home. The homeowner worked for the LAPD. He told us with shoulders hunched that he had purchased the TV for his son, who had terminal leukemia. It was his kid's dying wish was to have a big color TV set. This one, a common model of the day, was big and heavy, encased in a wooden cabinet, so stealing it was no small feat. The poor kid was distraught.

Unfortunately, we never recovered the TV. Soon after, I was in the Whittier courthouse for a case where I had to testify, and I saw the LAPD officer with a suitcase. "What are you doing here?" I asked him.

"When my son died, my wife went crazy," He told me. He had to have her committed. "These are her clothes. I'm on my way to visit her at the mental hospital."

Stranger than Strange

We saw crazy way to often! We never knew what we'd come across as deputies. People have some weird fetishes. I got a call one time about a suspicious man going through Dixie dumpsters behind the stores. He was collecting used tampons because he was turned on by them somehow. It takes all kinds.

Homicide Is Never Glamorous

The Department of State Hospitals-Metropolitan at Norwalk Boulevard and Bloomfield Avenue provided psychiatric care for those with mental health concerns. It had an open campus within a security perimeter so that patients could wander the premises almost like students on a college campus; only they were all medicated and under supervision. Around that time, there was a revolution in mental health facilities, with fewer beds and a push toward more humane treatment. But the state hospital was still like *One Flew Over the Cuckoo's Nest*, which was set in 1963.

I got a call about a patient who died. The remains were in the part of the building reserved for the severely mentally disturbed, which was on 24-7 lock-down. This lady was eating and choked on a piece of meat and died.

When I arrived on the ward, I was greeted by a nurse who looked like she could have been a professional wrestler. She certainly could take care of business if she needed to. I followed her, passing through a big common room. There were a bunch of ladies sitting on couches. One older woman sat there rocking a baby doll in her arms back and forth. She glanced up at me with glossy, far-away eyes and then focused back on the doll. It was haunting. I didn't like calls to the mental hospital.

71

Another time, I had a call about a suicide there. This time, the deceased was an employee. The guy was scheduled to go on a two-week vacation but got into a car accident before he was set to leave. He was at fault and had no insurance. I learned that he had also struggled with depression. We didn't know much about that back in the '60s. The employee lived in a room on the grounds in a different building than the patients. The staff thought he had left for vacation and locked his room until he returned.

When he didn't return after vacation, they unlocked his room to clean it and were greeted with a horrific smell. It was a particularly warm summer, over 100 degrees. They called 911, and I was the first responder. The guy had put a plastic bag over his head and hanged himself from a door jamb. He'd been there a while and had swelled up like a balloon. His bodily fluids had run out all over the floor.

I called the Homicide Department. In the case of a homicide, you don't touch the body. You don't even look for identification. You wait for the homicide officers. That's SOP, standard operating procedure. I was glad for the protocol. Gagging from the smell, I escaped outside onto the balcony and almost threw up. I avoided the room until the homicide detectives arrived.

When they showed up, I led them to the scene. "Oh shit," said one of the officers. When he cut him down, the corpse hit the floor hard and more liquid oozed out. It was like stepping on a ripe grape. It was terrible. They were going to have to shovel out the mess.

"How do you handle this?" I asked the guy from homicide. Back at the station later, I could still smell the stench on my uniform. I wanted to burn it.

"I put Vick's VapoRub under my nose," he said.

Working homicide may seem glamorous on TV shows, but it's ugly. To give you an idea, in another case, a man killed his employer. He cut his boss into pieces and took him to the San Gabriel Mountains where he dropped the body parts into outhouse pit toilets. The guys from homicide had to wear fishing waders to remove the parts. That's the reality of homicide.

My friend John Flaherty in homicide shared with me in the locker room about a case he was struggling with. "I've got a problem, and I don't know what to do. I've got a man, thirty-eight years old. His wife had a baby two months ago. But he was seeing a girlfriend on the side and died having sex with her."

He shook his head. "How do I clean it up?"

"You don't clean it up," I suggested. "I would give the wife the basics, and if she wants more information, tell her straight out."

Following their work at the crime scene, the homicide guys are often called to observe autopsies to get information about the cause of death and other details of the event. It's tough. We used to say that instead of going to a wedding, we went to the aftermath of a shooting at a wedding. When we were called to a party, there was blood, not punch.

I made one call where three kids got into a freezer, got locked in, and died. We responded to people who had shot themselves and their intestines were all over the ground, people who had cut themselves and blood was everywhere, parties where people had overdosed, and car accidents with people cut in half or decapitated. We saw shootings, suicides, child abuse, animal neglect, domestic violence, bar fights, and violent people.

How do those working in law enforcement handle all this? Some of them can't. It's too much after a while. That's why so many police officers become alcoholics, especially when they retire. Every day, they see some of the saddest and most gruesome aspects of humanity, and there's nothing they can do about it other than lock up the perpetrator.

I was right in there. I wrote a lot of dead body reports, but I didn't become an alcoholic. I had affection and support from my third and final wife, Dona, who was the love of my life for forty-five years. I also tried to have a sense of humor, and I always focused on the mission of my job: helping people.

CHAPTER 5

The Right to Remain Silent

W E'VE ALL HEARD IT IN *LAW AND ORDER* and every police show on TV—the Miranda Rights:

> "You have the right to remain silent. Anything you say can and will be used against you in a court of law. You have a right to an attorney. If you cannot afford an attorney, one will be appointed for you."

The Miranda Decision came down in the early 1960s, and it all began with a 24-year-old low-life drug user from Arizona named Ernesto Miranda. His interrogating officer called him Ernie. Ernie was arrested in 1963, on charges of kidnapping, rape, and robbery. He attacked an 18-year-old girl while she waited for a bus to take her home from her job at a movie theater, dragged her into his car, tied her hands, forced her to lie down in the backseat of the car, drove her twenty minutes to a spot outside the city, and raped her. Then, he took her money, forced her to lie in the back seat again, drove her back into the city, dropped her off a few blocks from her house, and sped off. The young lady reported the crime to the cops and gave them a description of Ernie. A few days later, the girl and her cousin noticed a car cruising slowly at the same bus stop where Ernie had taken her, and they reported the license plate to the police. The police ran the plates and traced them to a 29-year-old woman named Twilla Hoffman. Ernie was her live-in boyfriend, and they found him at her house. The officers asked him if he could come down to the station for a lineup. He said, "Yeah, no problem." At the lineup, the young woman identified him, and the cops pulled him out and took him for interrogation.

MIRANDA WARNING

1. YOU HAVE THE RIGHT TO REMAIN SILENT.
2. ANYTHING YOU SAY CAN AND WILL BE USED AGAINST YOU IN A COURT OF LAW.
3. YOU HAVE THE RIGHT TO TALK TO A LAWYER AND HAVE HIM PRESENT WITH YOU WHILE YOU ARE BEING QUESTIONED.
4. IF YOU CANNOT AFFORD TO HIRE A LAWYER, ONE WILL BE APPOINTED TO REPRESENT YOU BEFORE ANY QUESTIONING IF YOU WISH.
5. YOU CAN DECIDE AT ANY TIME TO EXERCISE THESE RIGHTS AND NOT ANSWER ANY QUESTIONS OR MAKE ANY STATEMENTS.

WAIVER

DO YOU UNDERSTAND EACH OF THESE RIGHTS I HAVE EXPLAINED TO YOU? HAVING THESE RIGHTS IN MIND, DO YOU WISH TO TALK TO US NOW?

When Ernie asked Captain Cooley, who was in charge, how he did at the lineup, the captain replied, "Not too good, Ernie." Ernie was probably anxious as they interrogated him for the next two hours without a lawyer. In the end, he confessed to the crime. The young woman was brought into the room, and Ernie agreed she was the woman he had raped. The girl agreed that his voice matched the voice of the man who had raped her. Also, his confession matched closely the testimony of the girl. And with that, the cops figured it was a slam dunk.

When Ernie was done confessing, he agreed to sign a document that said, "This confession was made with full knowledge of my legal rights, understanding any statement I made may be used against me." He was then sent to trial and convicted solely on his confession.

Ernie's 73-year-old court-appointed lawyer, Alvin Moore, tried to exclude Ernie's confession as evidence during the trial, arguing that his client's statement was not made voluntarily, and he was not provided with all the safeguards and rights afforded to him in the Constitution. He pointed out that Ernie had not been fully advised of his rights, including the right to remain silent or to have an attorney present for his interrogation. Alvin was overruled. Ernie was given 20 to 30 years in prison on both charges, and that might've been the end of it. But it wasn't.

Most court-appointed lawyers didn't go as far for their clients as Alvin Moore. Ernie was lucky to get him. Alvin was relentless. He appealed the case to the Arizona Supreme Court, but the confession and the conviction were upheld. That might've been the end of it. But it still wasn't.

Though Alvin became too ill to represent Ernie any further, the ACLU had become aware of the case. Two attorneys, John J. Flynn and John P. Frank, agreed to handle the case pro bono, and in November of 1965, the U.S. Supreme Court agreed to hear Ernie's case in *Miranda v. Arizona*. The ACLU lawyers said their client's rights had been violated because he had not been advised of his right to remain silent before or during questioning. They added that an "emotionally disturbed man like Miranda, with limited education, should not be expected to be aware of his right not to incriminate himself."

The lawyer for the state of Arizona argued that if criminals were aware of their rights before interrogation, it would obstruct public safety. If a criminal is going to incriminate himself, why not let him? To be fair, if Ernie had known that he didn't have to confess, he would have kept his mouth shut, and the young woman may never have gotten justice. As DNA testing and other forms of evidence were unavailable back then, it would have been her word against his.

Ultimately, the Supreme Court ruled in favor of Ernie, and his conviction was overturned. After that, officers were issued Miranda warning cards that they were required to read to perps during arrest or before an interrogation. But here's the thing: the Miranda warning had always existed, just not in an official form. Early in my career as a deputy, before we started any interrogation, we had to say, "Everything you say or do will be used against you in a court of law." But before the Miranda hearing, there was a lot of controversy about it. When did we need to say it? Did we have to say the whole thing? Did we have to say it in a certain way? Members of law enforcement used their discretion. I'm pretty sure some cops didn't say it at all. The ruling in 1965 clarified the issue, which was better in my book.

But after the ruling, it took months for the Supreme Court to decide what we should say and when. We couldn't understand why it took them so long. Even though very few of us deputies and sergeants had college degrees and clearly weren't as educated as the judges on the Supreme Court, we knew how to make decisions quickly, on the spot. It was part of our job. And, while they figured it out, we were still making arrests, hoping that we were advising the suspects of their rights at the right time and in the right way. It was frustrating. During those months, some guys were kicked loose after arrest because the Miranda decision applied retroactively.

As for Ernesto Miranda, in 1967, he was retried without his confession and again convicted. His girlfriend testified against him that time. She told the court that he had confessed the rape to her. He was re-sentenced for 20 to 30 years, and justice was served.

The case made the name Miranda famous. When he was paroled in 1972, Ernie sold autographed Miranda warning cards for $1.50. He eventually got stabbed and killed in a bar fight. The police arrested the man they suspected of handing the knife to the guy who stabbed Miranda, but the suspect invoked his Miranda rights and refused to speak. Without any evidence, the cops had to release him. Because of his landmark court case, Ernie's killer was never found.

CHAPTER 6

The Watts Riot

THE SAME YEAR THE MIRANDA RIGHTS came into being, I made so many arrests that the procedure became second nature right away. The majority of the arrests were made—for better or worse—at the Watts Riot of 1965, sometimes called the Watts Rebellion or Uprising.

The Riot started over a drunk driving arrest by a California Highway Patrol motorcycle officer on August 11. He arrested a 21-year-old Black man named Marquette Frye for reckless driving when the young man failed to pass a field sobriety test. The officer called for a car to take Marquette to be booked in the county jail and a tow truck to impound Marquette's Buick, which belonged to his mother.

It should have been routine, but here's where the CHP screwed up big time: the passenger in the Buick, Marquette's brother, Ronald, was allowed to walk to his house nearby and bring their mother, Rena Price, back to the scene of the arrest.

Rena told off her son for driving drunk but didn't want the officers to take him away. "You ain't taking Marquette! You ain't taking him!" she yelled. She and Ronald helped Marquette resist arrest. A crowd gathered to watch the scene, and the situation quickly escalated. Reports say that someone shoved Rena, Marquette was struck in the face with a baton, Rena jumped an officer, and another officer pulled out a shotgun.

In the meantime, it went around that the police had roughed up Marquette. A rumor also spread that the police had kicked a pregnant woman. The growing number of spectators began yelling and throwing objects at the officers. I think years of mistrust, anger and oppression were all bubbling up. Finally, all three members of the Price family were arrested and taken away in a police car, but the dynamic of group unrest had already taken hold along Avalon Boulevard. It was a chaotic mess.

Riots erupted. For six days, Watts burned. People set fire to buildings in their own neighborhood. They resisted the police and threw rocks and bottles. There was vandalism, explosions, theft, and injuries.

Watts burning, 1965

On the day the uprising started, I was responding to a call at Harvey Aluminum at 190th and Western in Torrance, where there was a union strike. While we were there, we received a 1022 call, which meant to disregard the call we were on because we were needed elsewhere. The officer in charge, Paul Stumpy Stroben, told us, "Forget about Harvey. We're going to the riot." He walked up to the head of the union and said, "Knock it off. If we come back, you're all going to jail." The strike at Harvey Aluminum stopped, at least for a while. In 1967, the company and the United Steelworkers of America Union went to court for arbitration.

We sped north towards Watts in our patrol car, sirens blaring. I could see smoke from building fires rising into the sky ahead of us. I was one of probably seventy deputies early on the scene trying to keep the peace. Few of us had received any riot training. I had none, so there was a lot to learn on the fly. Later on, when I was on the SWAT team, I was given intense riot training, but that was after the Watts Riot.

A colleague of mine at the riot

For the next two weeks, we worked twelve-hour days. It was exhausting. I'd go home and sleep for six hours, then report back to Watts, patrolling from 6:00 p.m. at night until 6:00 a.m. in the morning. LAPD brought out their mobile kitchen. At 4:00 a.m. in the morning, my partner and I would take a needed break and sit there eating barbecued

steaks and green-tinged eggs made from powder. Hey, we were
hungry, and everything tastes good at four in the morning after
working for ten hours, and it was free!

We made
hundreds of arrests,
mostly for robbery.
There was a lot
of looting, people
stealing armfuls of
merchandise from
stores. We didn't have
enough handcuffs
to accommodate
the mass arrests and
were instructed to use
flex cuffs, which are
basically heavy-duty
plastic zip ties.

Looting in Watts

I did my best
to keep the peace,
trying to ensure that people weren't being victimized and that
things didn't get further out of control. Mostly, we were there
to show our presence and arrest the bad guys, and people doing
bad things, while helping the good people. There was a high
percentage of good people in Watts. They were good people
forced into a crummy situation because of government-sanctioned
residential segregation. Look at Proposition 14, passed in 1964,
which overturned the Rumford Fair Housing Act of 1963. The
proposition legally allowed property sellers, landlords, and their
agents to openly discriminate on racial or ethnic grounds when
selling or renting accommodations. That was one of many racially
discriminatory laws that existed at the time.

During the Riots, people were doing crazy things. One of my
partners who was Black told one perpetrator, "You guys are putting

By the end of the riot, there was 40 million dollars in damage, and almost 1,000 buildings were damaged and destroyed.

us in an even harder position—you're disgracing me and my race." He didn't like it. He didn't like it at all. He felt like it was setting things back.

People were understandably frustrated with their situation in Watts, including a lack of jobs and opportunities. It was a vicious cycle, and Watts had become a high-crime area. Businesses were hesitant to establish themselves there. When a Walmart opened in the area, it was robbed frequently. Businesses could only survive if they invested in security. Most new industrial buildings had few windows. Goodyear invested in a Tire Company at 56th and Central, with barely a window and with two security guards out front. As a result, it did well.

The pranking between law enforcement officers usually didn't extend to the general public, but I think my colleagues were getting punchy and tired at Watts. During one arrest, guy was coming out of a store with a huge armful of clothes right in front of me. I aimed my gun between his eyes to make the point that he was busted and also because you never knew if someone was carrying. I relieved him of the stolen merchandise and was about to flex-cuff him when a deputy behind him lit a firecracker, and it went off with a sharp BANG. The man fell to the ground and defecated in his pants. He thought he had died. Gunshots were going off all the time during the riot. It scared the shit out of him—literally. It happened so quickly that I didn't know what was going on at first. When I realized what had happened, I started laughing along with the deputy who had pulled the prank. It wasn't how I wanted it to go down, and it obviously wasn't funny for the perp. I think we just desperately needed a release from the tension round us. When he got to the jail, we made sure the man could get all cleaned up.

The shoot-out during the riot

During the riot, the Sheriff's Department served alongside the LAPD and the Highway Patrol. Every agency had a little bit of a different culture, a different way of doing things, and different on-the-job training. On the third night, the L.A. Chief of Police, William Parker, called Governor Pat Brown and asked for a "paramilitary" response to the disorder. The Governor publicly and dramatically declared that law enforcement was confronting "guerrillas fighting with gangsters" and called in the National Guard. Suddenly, 2,300 guardsmen were on site. The first riot-related death occurred that night when a Black civilian was killed in the crossfire during a shoot-out between the Guard and rioters.

In another incident I heard about from my partners, locals had put up a sign at 102nd and Grade Street that said: "Turn left and get shot." A man driving a black Cadillac ran the blockade. The National Guard opened up on him with a 30-caliber machine gun and killed the guy. In response, the rioting spread to other areas of Southern California. It was like a wildfire. It felt unreal at times. The riot started on a Wednesday; by Saturday, 16,000 law enforcement personnel mobilized and patrolled the city.

Interacting with the National Guard

Despite the craziness of the event, I never fired a shot. I didn't see anyone brutalized, but many people went to jail. There was a lot of damage, a lot of loss. Afterward, the estimates were that

The sign put up by locals

nearly 33,000 adults had participated in the riots. Many more were "sympathetic, but not active," and over the first six days—the worst of it—there were 34 deaths, 1,032 injuries, 3,438 arrests, and over $40 million in property damage. Despite the Governor's declaration, the vast majority of those arrested had no prior criminal record. Of the 34 deaths, three were "sworn personnel," and all were accidents: a firefighter struck by falling debris, a deputy sheriff killed by another deputy during a struggle with rioters, and a Long Beach police officer shot by another officer during a scuffle.

A minor side effect was that all the fires and fire damage led to long-term insurance problems. For my modest house in Whittier, my fire insurance costs $80 for three years up until then. After the riots, it tripled, going up to $80 a year. The major effect was that following the Watts Uprising, everything became more difficult for the people of that neighborhood, and there was a feeling of heightened social tension all over the country.

CHAPTER 7

Santa Barbara Station

WITH THE MONEY I WAS MAKING AS A DEPUTY, my wife and I sold our starter home and bought a nicer home in Whittier in a great neighborhood. It was an attempt to keep the marriage together. We put a 20-foot by 40-foot pool in the backyard, using a contractor that a fellow deputy recommended. The pool had cantilever decking with a diving board. Two other deputies built a big chain link fence around it. It was beautiful.

I tried to be a good guy to my wife. I was celibate after the affair with my fellow deputy, but things continued to fall apart. We went to marriage counseling to no avail. Finally, she told me she wanted a divorce. We filed and that was that. In 1967, I transferred from the L.A. Sheriff's Department to the Santa Barbara Sheriff's Department to get away from her. It was time for a change. I took my clothes, a few belongings, some guns I had collected, a V.W. bug and left. After eleven years, that's all I had. I slept on a friend's floor for a few days until I found a place to live.

But it was a relief. I felt free in a way that I had never felt before. We had married when we were so young and had grown apart years before. It had gotten to the point where we were saying terrible things to each other. She said I was fat. I called her a tramp. We both were seeing people on the side. It was awful.

I know the divorce was hard on the kids, but we did our best to make it work for them. Luckily, I had my days with them and moved into a big house with a buddy where I could host them. It was a white two-story home with an upper veranda and big picture windows on forty-seven acres in Montecito, right on the water, located next to the Four Seasons Biltmore Hotel. Just gorgeous. It had an amazing view of the Channel Islands.

It helped that my ex and I could sell the house in Whittier and split the profits. My share from the sale of the house was about six grand. I started paying alimony and child support. My ex-wife dated a couple of guys before eventually remarrying and moving to Tarzana, north of the San Fernando Valley, until her husband died of cancer. She has since remarried.

The house in Montecito

The front of our house in Montecito

I was only 31 years old. Other than supporting my kids and estranged wife, I didn't have a lot of expenses. My salary had been steadily increasing with my years in the force. I was up to about $6,000 a year. That's equivalent to about $50,000 now, which went farther in those days. I realized I had to take care of myself. I had to look out for myself since I was alone. So, I decided to treat myself. The same deputy who had referred the pool contractor to me had a connection with a Porsche dealer in Hollywood named Rudolf Absel, who owned Tourist Cars International. Originally from Amsterdam, Holland, during World War II Rudolph had been part of the underground helping the Americans. He was a straight shooter. He sold me an imported '69 Porsche 912, a four-cylinder with a special green-gold paint job. It was a gorgeous car. I loved it. And it wasn't bad to have when it came to attracting women.

I also went to the Garment District in Los Angeles and bought a quality luggage set and a Lucien Piccard gold watch from a really wonderful guy I knew named Maury. Maury had survived the Nazi death camp at Auschwitz during World War II. He still had the I.D. number tattooed on his arm. Auschwitz-Birkenau was the

88

only extermination camp that tattooed its prisoners. It was widely known that buying in the Garment District afforded discounts you couldn't get in the stores, and Maury gave me a great deal. On top of that, I got the "police price." We never paid full price for anything. It was a good perk to the job.

Me and my Porsche

Working a Beach Town

My other reason for leaving Norwalk was a sergeant that had it in for me. He didn't like me because I was not military trained, and he was an ex-Marine. He had also been my sergeant at the academy. He showed his displeasure there, too. He tended to give me a rough time and was critical of my reports, which I took a lot of care in writing. At the Santa Barbara Sheriff's Department, I was told I could take a promotional exam and move up in rank quickly. That sounded good, so I left the L.A. department to work two and a half hours north in Santa Barbara and commuted when I went to pick up my kids.

I was well-received in Santa Barbara, a pretty beach town with a university nearby, but not much was happening there. It was so quiet compared to Norwalk and what I was used to. We went five days without a call! Within our jurisdiction was Montecito, home of the wealthy and famous. Oprah Winfrey lives there. We made our rounds through the neighborhood but weren't called there much, although once we responded to an urgent call involving a fatality. A young man had recently graduated from college and moved back home. His parents told him, "You're off the free path. You need to get a job." He killed himself in front of his girlfriend. He ate his gun. It was an ugly sight. The girl was understandably traumatized.

People commit suicide in weird ways. One guy, who was sadistic, put a little water in his shotgun when he killed himself so that his brains and blood splattered all over the ceiling and walls and dripped down on the officers.

Other than that, I only have one or two interesting cases worth recollecting from my stint in Santa Barbara. One was a call about a home intruder with a troubling conclusion. The thief had entered the house while the lady who lived there was at home. She had a gun, but she didn't want to kill the guy—she only wanted to stop him. So, she shot him in the arm. The burglar was rushed to the hospital, but the damage to his arm made it unusable. The bullet had cut the tendons. His arm was like a paperweight. He went to jail for breaking and entering and attempted robbery. When he got out of prison, he began harassing the woman and her family, blaming her for his bum arm and threatening to sue until they had to sell their house and move. The lady thought she was doing the right thing but that didn't turn out so great.

Could he have sued her? California is a Stand Your Ground Law state, which means you have the right to defend yourself and your property and do not need to simply try to run away. But the law has stipulations, like using "proportional "or "reasonable" force, which are defined in pages of legalize. In this case, I don't think the woman would've been held responsible, but the harassment was enough to make them pack their bags.

The Packers

We regularly checked on the bars in Santa Barbara and the college town of Isla Vista, including a classic college bar called The Brothers, The Green Bay Packers were in town, training at the University of California at Santa Barbara stadium for the 1967 Super Bowl and their showdown with the Kansas City Chiefs. The players were in The Brothers, having drinks and dancing with girls; Bart Starr, Lionel Aldrich, Donny Anderson, Jim Grabowski, and Willie Davis were among them. The media likes to focus on sports stars misbehaving, but I was pleased to witness all the men acting like gentlemen and engaging in only stand-up behavior.

That was my last call in Santa Barbara. I'd served there for several months and finally received word that instead of being able to take the promotional exam right away, I'd have to wait a couple of years. That being the case, I made some inquiries and was able to return to Los Angeles and keep all my seniority at the East L.A. Sheriff's Station. I wouldn't return to Isla Vista until 1970 to keep the peace at a series of riots with serious consequences for the peacekeepers.

CHAPTER 8

East Los Angeles Station, 1967–1968

I LOVED SERVING AT THE EAST L.A. STATION. Good people worked there. When I first arrived, I was assigned early mornings, and the tradition on Sunday mornings was to serve menudo to everyone at the station. We bought it at a restaurant near the handball courts where we played after work sometimes. Menudo is a spicy Mexican red chili pepper soup made with tripe, which is the stomach lining of a pig. Hominy, lime, onions, and oregano are used to season the broth. We'd buy two gallons for the station every Sunday to recover from whatever we'd done on Saturday night because menudo is supposed to be good for

hangovers. I don't know about that, but people seemed to appreciate the tradition.

My superiors thought highly of me. They made me a two-striper within two months of my return—the rank below sergeant. This made me a lightweight supervisor and a training officer for new deputies. Incidentally, that would remain my rank until retirement. So, I started training other guys. As a result, I had a lot of partners during that time.

Training Newbies

One of my first trainees was Leroy Baca, who became Los Angeles County Sheriff from 1998 to 2014. Leroy was a Marine Corps Reserve Officer and had a Ph.D. Among his accomplishments as sheriff, he pushed for inmate education initiatives, fought homelessness, and promoted religious tolerance. Unfortunately, he was also tied to covering up anti-Semitic remarks by Mel Gibson and to Paris Hilton's early release. According to court reports, in 2011 he was involved in obstructing U.S. Immigration and Customs Enforcement and lying to the FBI during an investigation of inmate abuses in the county jail system. In 2017, at the age of 77 and suffering from Alzheimer's, he was convicted on felony charges and jailed for three years.

Leroy, who was only 25 at the time, and I were patrolling together for just a few days in the standard squad car of the time, either a Plymouth Fury or Ford four-door. Working after midnight into the daylight, we regularly stopped at this Mexican restaurant on Soto and Olympic Blvd at 2:00 in the morning where I routinely ordered a double-wrapped bean and cheese burrito.

Driving away from the restaurant on one shift, we saw a guy passed out in the street in the middle of Olympic and Atlantic, a corner with heavy traffic. We stopped the car in the road with lights flashing to protect him. It was clear when we examined him that the guy had overdosed on drugs. We carefully rolled him over, and suddenly he had a moment of consciousness and tried to hit Leroy. Well, that was a mistake. Leroy hit him back with a Gonzales 415 sap, a blackjack with a lead ingot internal frame covered by layers of leather. It broke the suspect's cheekbone. We took him in custody to the hospital and arrested him on charges of assault on a police officer and heroin possession.

Leroy asked me later, "Are we in trouble?" I said, "No, we took care of it. It's no problem." Leroy was unexperienced. He felt threatened and reacted. If it had been me, I would've just turned the guy over and handcuffed him. But what was done, was done. Now, had used that kind of physical force with someone just mouthing off, I would've got on him and try to teach him better.

My next trainee was Bill Kush, an ex-Chicago cop who could write brilliant reports. As partners, we were assigned security for Teddy Kennedy, who was unveiling a new rehab center in East L.A. To fit in with the crowd, we wore plain clothes—a couple of cheap suits. We met up with Kennedy beforehand for our briefing, but he never thanked or acknowledged us. It made him seem arrogant. That was my first VIP security duty.

Later, when I was working security for Ronald Reagan, Governor of California at the time, he approached us, shook our

Ted Kennedy, 1967 and Ronald and Nancy Reagan, 1972

hands, and said thank you. I appreciated that. Along with those two, I worked security for other VIPs. One was an event featuring President Nixon. I wasn't assigned directly to him though. However, in 1978 I was on the security team for the mayor of Jerusalem, Tedd Kollek, when he was speaking at UCLA. I was briefed by the Secret Service. Training included inspecting manholes and testing food that would be served to the VIP. I still have a confidential booklet from the Secret Service about protecting presidents.

Generally, when I was training deputies, I changed partners every two weeks or so. My next partner, George Reed, was a brilliant guy. George grew up in South America and spoke fluent Spanish, which was helpful in the field. When we apprehended two burglary suspects and were driving them back to the station, while they conversed in Spanish in the back seat, George understood every word. After we booked them, we knew just where to go to recover the stolen property. George eventually became a captain. His wife, a sheriff's deputy, was also on the force. Sadly, they both died prematurely. They were returning from Las Vegas on his lieutenant's private plane when it crashed in the fog near Santa Clarita, and everyone was killed.

Working with a deputy named Art Palino, we saved a detective's life one night. It was a cruise night in Whittier and we joined the line of cruising cars. Most of the traffic was going in the opposite direction. We were checking out the scene on either side of the street and as we passed an old, closed movie theater across the street, I saw a fight taking place by the ticket booth under the marquee. I recognized one of the guys in the fight as a plainclothes detective named Harry Buds. He wore a cheap suit to blend into whatever action he was surveying.

We immediately pulled over and ran across the road just as the other guy in the fight grabbed Harry's gun. I hit this guy with an uppercut and watched little white bits fly out of his mouth. They were his front teeth. With that and at Art's gunpoint, he dropped the weapon. There were drugs all over the ground around it.

As Harry cuffed him, I asked, "Where's your partner?" I suspected he wasn't alone. The guy mumbled that he was around the corner. We arrested his accomplice in the getaway car, too. When Harry returned to the station at the end of our shift, he said, "Bob, I owe you my life. That guy was going to kill me. I owe you." But he didn't owe me. I was following the code. We always made sure that we protected each other.

Art eventually transferred to Gorman Station on Highway 5 near Frazier Park. As he was placing a man under arrest for a simple traffic warrant, the suspect took his gun and killed him. There may have been a struggle, or he made a mistake. Who knows? There is sometimes a big price to pay for being a cop: It can cost you your life.

After I trained many other guys, Don Swift became my permanent partner. He was at the top of his training class at the academy, a smart guy who happened to have perfect penmanship when writing up reports. He worked as a clerk for the FBI before joining the Sheriff's Department. He and I were not only great as partners, but we also became great friends for over fifty years.

I had some terrific partners in my career. There was only one partner who I didn't like and didn't trust—no one liked him. He was self-centered. It was his way or no way. He wore a lot of jewelry and loved to bullshit. He didn't like working with others and was downright mean, talking down to everyone and acting as if he was superior. I met him toward the end of my career when I was doing fugitive detail, transporting fugitive suspects from other states back to California and vice versa. I had to work with him occasionally, but I kept it low-key when I did.

With all of my other partners, I never had a problem. We always took care of each other. It's the same rule in the squad car with a partner as they say about Las Vegas—whatever happens there stays there. You might share stuff with your partner or vice versa, and it was understood that it was completely confidential.

When filling out reports about our calls, I wrote down how it happened. Whatever my partner and I said we did, that was the Gospel truth. I don't care if God asked me, the story never changed.

Patrol Cars

Before we went out on patrol, checking out the squad car for dents and its general condition was important. Nobody wanted to get blamed for dents that were already there. It was like inspecting a rental car. For obvious reasons, you wanted to ensure the vehicle was in good working condition. One day, I was inspecting my assigned car and hit the brakes to test them. The pedal went to the floor before bringing the car to a halt. I walked back into the station.

"Hey, Sarge, the pedal goes all the way to the floor."

"Pump the brakes," he said.

"Wait a minute. You want me to take out a car with bad brakes?" I thought for a second. "Okay, give me a note saying you told me to take this car. If I have a problem, it's on you. It's on your shoulders."

He frowned at me. "Oh, all right, take the lieutenant's car."

Sometimes, you had to advocate for yourself. Everyone was busy, and resources were limited.

It was also important to check for contraband in the backseat when starting a patrol and after transporting a suspect. One time, we hooked up a man for drunk driving. As usual, we took him to the county jail in the back of the squad car in handcuffs. We got him into the jail and booked. Afterward, I checked the back seat. The guy had hidden some heroin between the seat cushions. I went back into the jail with the stash, and we booked him on an additional charge of possession.

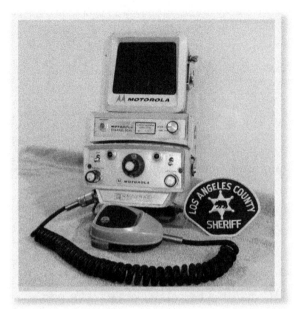

Car radio system, 1960s and 70s.

Dispatch Calls in East L.A.

It took me a while to get the hang of the codes and dispatch calls when I first started as a deputy, but by the time I was working in East L.A., it was second nature. In training for patrol, we never used words. We used numbers because dispatchers had to move fast. You wouldn't believe the number of calls the dispatchers received, sometimes handling two stations with twenty or thirty cars each. They had to be sharp. And everything had to be communicated quickly. For example: "211 now, shots fired. 901 physicians, 1021 watch commander." Or in shorthand without numbers: "Robbery now. Shots fired. Ambulance responding. Call the watch commander." Dispatchers had to know what they were doing, and our dispatchers were excellent.

We didn't have the computer system we have now. Each station had a unique number code. Temple Station was 4; Lennox was 3; Firestone was 1; and Malibu was 10. Each jurisdiction had a unique number, and each squad car had its own. If they were broadcasting the address of an incident, say 415 Boyle Street, the dispatcher had to know which jurisdiction the neighborhood was in and which squad car was in charge of patrolling that area. They couldn't send a car from across town, which could result in having deputies who didn't know the neighborhood and got there too late to help. If we were busy with a prisoner in custody or on another call, they'd give an incident in our area to the car in the adjoining area.

If we wanted a quicker return on a stolen vehicle, we'd try to get the license plate number and call it in, saying our car number first and then the message with the license plate number, such as 21, Adam Boy Charles (ABC) 123, and it's rolling—meaning it's moving. The dispatcher Once, when that happened, the dispatcher said, "10-4, 21. How did you get a rolling I.D.?" I said, "Very difficult." Then, I had to explain to her that I was teasing. The car was stationary. It was nearly impossible to I.D. a moving stolen vehicle back then.

Force and Fear

Probably the worst common call we received was "211 now." The full call from a dispatcher might sound something like: "211 now, 923, 901 physicians, 20 SAM, 22 assist, 23 assist, 1021 for location, 21 handle, robbery now, shots fired, ambulance responding and other cars responding, and the sergeant responding. Call the watch commander."

In 1968, a California Penal Code Section 211 was defined as a robbery with "force and fear," meaning there had to be a weapon of force involved, usually a gun, and the victim had to be afraid for their life. We didn't want to get a 211 call because we knew something heavy was going down. Someone was seriously injured. It could be ugly. When a 211 came in, we immediately got jacked up and were ready for anything as we sped to the scene.

And we had to get wherever we were going fast, which meant we had to know the neighborhoods we patrolled backward and forward: what side of the street were the even-numbered and odd-numbered addresses, the quickest route to get from A to B, where specific businesses and bars were located, and school zones to avoid. We always had to have an accurate map in our heads.

Force and fear—both of those elements had to be involved

to make it a 211 crime, a felony-level offense that could result in a substantial prison sentence. But if no force was established, the penalty was reduced to a misdemeanor or could get dismissed all together.

This came into play once when I was on the stand in court as the arresting officer of this little gangster who robbed a truck driver at gunpoint. The victim, the trucker, was a big guy, built like a refrigerator.

The judge asked him, "Did the suspect have a gun?"

"Yes, your honor," he replied.

"Were you afraid?"

"No, I wasn't afraid of that guy. He's a little punk."

The judge dismissed the case because, though there was force, there was no element of fear.

Two weeks later, the state changed the definition of 211, Robbery, to force OR fear. Had the crime occurred two weeks later, the suspect would have been arrested and served time.

Laws and rulings of punishment were in constant flux. It was just another element of it all. Then there was the bending and loopholing of the law used often by defense attorneys. As an officer out on the street daily trying to keep people safe, I thought defense attorneys generally didn't care about us. They'd defend Lucifer if he paid them a large enough legal fee. For example, I arrested a sex offender who had abused several girls. The defense attorney argued, "Your Honor, my client is no longer a threat to society. He went for a psychiatric evaluation showing he'd been cured of this behavior and should be given probation."

If I were the judge in that case, I would've said, "Okay, Counselor, you say your client has been cured of this mischievous behavior. I want him to babysit your kids while you're gone as part of his probation, and we'll see what happens."

A Dreaded 996 Call

I was in Car 24 working in what we referred to as Area 24, a highly congested two-square-mile area in the western part of East L.A. near the Pomona Freeway when we got a rare call that made our hair stand on end, a "996." Dispatchers used "999" to mean that all cars from every station everywhere should proceed to an incident—Malibu, East L.A., Norwalk, Temple, Industry—all the stations. I never heard that one. A "997" was the call for all cars from our station: Officer Needs Help Urgently, District Cars Only (five units with shortest ETA to respond). That was bad too. And code "996" meant there was an explosion, and that often meant casualties.

The call that day sounded something like this: "996. 24 handle. 23 assist. 20 SAM. (Which meant the sergeant was rolling.) 1021 (that's the location). Call the watch commander." My partner and I glanced at each other as I hit the siren and we sped towards the location. We knew it was something big.

When we arrived at the scene, we found utter destruction and a horrifying sight. What was once a modest house in a struggling residential area was blown to bits. The man's yard and the street were full of debris. Windows of other homes were broken a block away from the explosion. One of the worst parts of the incident was that among the wreckage on the lawn, thrown about thirty feet, was the body of the man who lived there. He had a softball-sized hole in his chest.

With witness reports, we pieced together what happened. The man had been trying to put out a small brush fire outside his garage. We never found out how it started. Inside the garage was an acetylene tank used for arc welding, which leaked. It blew. Neighbors gathered around as we arrived. I called in for crowd control. After that, there was nothing to do but report a dead body, wait for the fire truck and ambulance, and write a ten-page report. Sometimes, you can't do anything.

Sometimes a call wasn't high-adrenaline. It was just sad. That was true for a duty called Death Notification, 919. We were trained for it but, thankfully, I never had to do one. Everyone hoped they would never have to do it. It meant when someone died away from home—a husband was killed in a traffic accident or a wife in an airplane accident, we had to show up at the front door to inform the rest of the family.

In training, they told us, "Don't go to the door and say, 'Hey, Barbara, your husband is dead.' Go to the next-door neighbor Phyllis first, tell her, and take her with you so she can comfort the new widow." However, as uniformed officers, we had to make the awful announcement, "Mrs. Jones, I'm sorry to tell you, but your husband died in an airplane accident in Detroit." That would make for a tough day for everyone involved. Because it was grim, there were naturally lots of jokes about it at the training academy as an antidote.

Helping on the Highway

The CHP took care of the roads and the traffic, and the Sheriff's Department took care of the criminals. Deputies didn't normally handle accidents, but when I was working a graveyard shift and a citizen approached me at two in the morning and said, "Hey, Deputy, there's a bad accident on the freeway," my partner and I, not involved in another call, went to check it out. The accident was near the Atlantic Boulevard exit on the Long Beach Freeway, a four-lane highway heading into L.A.

Two intoxicated men were changing a flat tire half on the shoulder and half on the freeway—which was stupid—when an eighteen-wheeler hit them. There were body parts two hundred yards down the road. One guy was split up the middle, as if he'd been cut in half with a chainsaw. It was unbelievable, the gore of that scene, just a mess. We called the CHP to respond.

In the meantime, we looked inside the car, and passed out in the back was another passenger. I woke him up. "Hey," I said, "Who are your partners?"

"You go ask them!" he said in a drunken slur.

"We can't. They're dead." That sobered him up right away! We talked to the truck driver, too. The only damage to the eighteen-wheeler was a small dent in the chrome bumper about the size of a baseball.

All-Too-Common Domestic Disputes

Way too frequently, we had to intervene in a family's affairs. The two most dangerous calls were domestic disputes and 919s, Keep the Peace. It was horrifying, the amount of violence we saw between spouses and among family members.

A Keep the Peace call was usually when a divorce was taking place and the husband or wife was in the process of moving out of the home. I had a couple of those while working in East L.A. There would be a serious amount of friction and animosity between the couple. Usually, the wife called in for help, saying something like, "My husband's violent. I've got a problem. I need some help."

My job in a 919 was to be there to oversee the process and make sure no one got hurt. This sometimes lasted three hours or more while the departing spouse carried everything to a truck or car. In the process, I shadowed the reluctant or potentially violent spouse all around the house. Everywhere they went, even to the bathroom, I was there. You never knew where they might stash a gun or knife. A husband could say he wanted to take a shower and come out with a revolver and shoot his wife. I wouldn't get in the shower with him, but I was there nearby. I had to be on my toes doing domestic calls, always.

During one graveyard shift, my partner and I got a family disturbance call at a residence where there were three previous calls for disturbing the peace. The dispatcher was tired of it. "Handle it to a conclusion," he said, "We've been there enough."

We could hear the fighting before we'd even gotten inside. Once we entered, we tried to calm the man. The woman who lived there was in the bathroom, and we waited for her to come out. Then while my back was turned away from the bathroom, she threw open the door and came at me her fist raised, holding a big pair of heavy fabric shears.

My partner saw it happening. With all his weight, he knocked her to the ground before she stabbed me. We hooked her up, arrested her for a 217 PC, Attempted Murder of a deputy, a felony that meant she was going to prison if convicted.

It was important to follow procedure when arresting women. When we took female suspects into custody, we were required to provide mileage from our location to the station. We'd say to the dispatcher, "21, 1015 with a female, mileage is 21,000 and 3/10ths" or something like that. Then the dispatcher would reply, "Okay, 21, the time is 11:45." That was an important standard operating procedure for a male deputy. You didn't want a problem in which the suspect accuses you of foul play, saying, "This guy didn't take me directly to the station. He took me out and 'boinked' me first." It was CYA, cover your backside.

I went to the scissor-stabbing woman's preliminary hearing at the courthouse in East L.A., which was located across from the East L.A. station with a pond between the two buildings. Perpetrators occasionally used to steal a car and drive it into the pond. As the hearing started, the DA read the report, changing the attempted murder charge to a 245, assault with a deadly weapon, still a felony. That was fine. But it turned out that the judge, Myer Marion, wanted to clear his calendar. It was the case of another judge acting like a god, knowing no one could touch him. He had the final say. That day, Judge Marion wanted to be done by noon so he could go to Santa Anita Race Track. He said, "Since Officer Mead wasn't hurt, we're going to make the charge a misdemeanor, a 415 PC, Disturbing the Peace, not a felony. There will be no preliminary hearing. The court fines the defendant $25."

So, she walked. True story. There were many fine and responsible judges for whom we had respect, but there were also judges like Marion for whom we had no respect.

As a result of another domestic dispute, I responded to a rescue call in East L.A. where the victim, a man, was cut in the femoral artery on his inner thigh. He was bleeding to death. The carotid artery on either side of the neck is the biggest in the human body. If that's cut, you die quickly. If you cut the femoral, you can also bleed to death in a pretty short amount of time, but not as quickly. This guy was going in and out of consciousness with the blood loss and was close to death when we arrived on the scene. The blood was dark, meaning it was draining from closer to the heart. I applied direct pressure on the wound until the ambulance arrived. When the EMTs took over, they put a tourniquet around his leg before whisking him away to the hospital, saying to me, "Good work, Deputy. You saved his life."

Later, in the hospital, I asked the victim what happened. "I cut myself shaving," he said, obviously not wanting to reveal what really happened. It turned out that his girlfriend caught him cheating and tried to whack off his privates and missed. She went for the goods. But he refused to testify against her. We even had the bloody knife in possession, a steak knife, six inches long with her fingerprints on it. He didn't want her to go to jail. So, we kissed it off and didn't even take a report. We left them to themselves to sort it out. It was a good argument in favor of divorce.

One evening, the dispatcher called me and my partner with a 925, Suspicious Circumstances at a private residence. The husband, a Latino man, greeted us at the door looking pale and weak. It became obvious talking to him that he was a good, upstanding person, and he was glad to see us.

"I've got a problem," he told us quietly. "My wife's crazy. She tried to kill me with rat poison. I was very sick. I don't know what to do about her." We entered the home and found the wife sitting in front of a TV that was barely working. A white line ran down the middle of the screen, and she stared at it. We didn't arrest her but instead took her into custody, reporting a 5150, WIC, Welfare Institution Code, and escorted her to the psych ward.

Man, did I learn firsthand that people don't always act right toward one another. Another time during a daytime shift, I got a call from neighbors complaining that someone was repeatedly banging on the garage door next door. We worked in one-man cars during the day—we always had two deputies in a car at night and early morning—so I headed over on my own.

It turned out that the banging was coming from inside the garage. I managed to break a lock on the outside and open the door where I found an older man, perhaps in his 70s, overheated and scared. He didn't look so hot. He explained that his grandson had locked him in the garage when he went to school. The boy's parents had died, and his grandfather was his next of kin. The old man was under the care of the boy, who was just a teenager. I don't know if the man had dementia or some other ailment, but the young man didn't want to have any problems with his grandfather, so he locked him in the garage on purpose to keep him there until he got home from school. When we found the kid, he told us he planned let his grandfather out after school. Somehow he didn't understand that you can't lock people up all day for no reason. It was endangerment. We made no arrests, but explained the health risk to his grandfather and legal ramifications for him if he did it again. Hopefully, the two of them worked it out after we intervened.

Very occasionally when we were short-staffed, I worked the desk at the station taking incoming calls. I was manning the phone when a lady called and said, "Our son is afraid of us. He's hiding in the bathroom. We just got him."

I said, "What do you mean, you just got him?"

"He's about six years old. We traded a car for him. Please do something."

It was a bizarre story, but there was no way to know what was going on without checking it out, so we sent out a patrol. Sure enough, somebody gave away a child in exchange for a car. We call child support services. You have to wonder how these people function. Why would anyone trade a child for a car or the other way around? I didn't hear the follow up, but likely drugs were involved.

Birth

It happens at least once in most police officer's careers: we're called upon to deliver a baby. My time came during and evening shift. A woman had gone into labor in her home by herself, and so she called 911. My partner Jimmy Green and I called for back up and were joined by Jimmy Cessaroni and his partner. I didn't know what the hell to do, so I was pleased that the other guys did most of the "heavy lifting" while I fetched hot water and towels and provided general support. This was before we used surgical gloves to protect from disease, so it was a messy affair, but we successfully assisted in the delivery of the baby. The two Jimmys even tied off the umbilical cord. Then, the ambulance arrived to take the woman and her newborn to the hospital. That one had a happy ending.

Was I trained for the task? Hell, no! That was the ultimate on-the-job training.

An Average Graveyard Shift

Anything and everything could happen on a graveyard shift. On a weeknight, we might get six or seven calls. On the weekends it was around ten with substantially more if there was a full moon, I kid you not. I remember we got 22 calls during a full moon Saturday night. On one shift when I was requested to babysit two dead bodies at a cemetery, victims of a gang slaying, until homicide arrived, I didn't have time for many more calls.

When not responding to a call, we'd patrol, looking for a "good shake," suspicious characters, behavior or circumstances, like if a car had its brights on, the driver could be drunk because eyes dilate from excessive drinking, requiring more light to see. Or if the back of a car was hanging low, it could mean there was heavy contraband in the trunk, like a safe or a stolen ATM machine.

Here's an example of the cases during one Friday night shift.

Drunks

The first call was about a drunk on the street causing disruption to the citizens living in that neighborhood. Almost every shift, we'd have to deal with drunk people misbehaving. Drunks were always more of a problem than drug users, be it marijuana or heroin or whatever. Booze makes people more aggressive and less conscious of consequences, that false "liquid courage." Drugs dumb down people. The heavier drugs put the users into a stupor in which they can't function. Drunks get into fights, can force themselves on women, can steal and vandalize, and make a lot of noise. Whether we hooked them up depended on the disruption level and whether they were breaking the law. If it was clear-cut criminal activity, we'd take them to the station. If not, we had to do something with them, especially when they wouldn't stop their disorderly conduct.

We put the disruptive drunk in the back of the car and dropped him off at the Hollenbeck LAPD station. That got rid of him, at least from our jurisdiction. We did this on occasion as a way to get some weight off of our shoulders. The PD sometimes did the same, dropping off drunks to us.

Non-Stop Wedding

We responded to another noise complaint at about one o'clock a.m. It came from a house where they were having a wedding reception. You could hear the music a block away, way too loud for

108

that time of night. When we entered the premises, I went straight to the stereo and unplugged the electrical cord.

"Who sent you?" said an angry drunk guy.

"God sent me," I said, then we talked to him about being courteous of his neighbors. Who knows if it sank in, but they didn't turn the music back on.

A Washer on His Johnson

"Person injured," was the next call. The fire department responded with us, and, yeah, we found a man injured, all right. The guy had put a metal washer around his Johnson. Why? Who knows! The man was a little strange. Of course, the penis expanded, and he couldn't get the washer off. By the time we got there, it had turned black and blue. It was quite an ugly sight. The fire department had to cut off the washer with bolt cutters, being careful not to whack off anything else. Honestly, I couldn't make up some of the strange things I saw people do.

Flipping for a .45

I was patrolling that night with my frequent partner, and friend Ray Lorne. We roomed together when I was still single. Our next call was for a drug arrest on Whittier Boulevard. Being a Friday night, it was cruise night with the low riders rolling slowly down the boulevard to show off their rides with music blasting from their stereos and raising and lowering their cars if they had hydraulics. We were patting down suspects on Whittier when Ray spotted a guy walking by and said, "He looks like a good shake. Let's pat him down." He was right. The guy was carrying a .45 handgun. We hooked him up for a concealed weapon and confiscated the gun as evidence.

Back in the sixties, when a case was terminated, a cop was given the weapon involved. The judge gave it to us, and Ray and I flipped for it. Ray won the toss and got the .45. Sadly, after he retired, Ray committed suicide. A lot of people had trouble handling all the shit we saw.

Up in the L.A. Alps

Next, the dispatcher requested our car to check some sort of crash and property damage in the hilly part of East L.A. that we called the Alps. With the usual flashing lights and siren, we pulled up to a restaurant. A car had lost its brakes, rolled down a hill, picked up speed, and crashed through the back of the place. The damaged car was wedged awkwardly inside the restaurant. Luckily, it was in the middle of the night on a Sunday and the restaurant was closed. Still, we worried about victims, but we couldn't get in or get at the car to see if anyone was trapped inside. An unhappy chow dog with a blue tongue was guarding the restaurant, tied to a fifteen-foot heavy metal chain. He barked and growled and leapt at us. We finally got a hold of the restaurant owner, who showed up, unlocked the dog's chain, and moved him into the parking lot, where he secured the dog to a chain link fence. We checked the inside of the vehicle but the driver wasn't there. And no one had been inside the building, which was a relief.

Then, before we knew it, as the owner walked away from the restaurant through the parking lot, he tripped over the dog's chain and fell to the ground. The startled animal went for his own owner's throat. The guy turned in time, so the dog bit him on the shoulder instead of the jugular vein, but he required medical treatment. In addition to reporting a hit and run, we had to call Animal Control. The owner asked us to put the dog down.

Along with those, there were the usual bar fights, domestic violence calls, and constant patrolling, just an average night of law enforcement in East L.A.

Another night in East L.A. A drug bust when the growing and possession of marijuana were illegal. Above, that's me holding the confiscated plant. And, right, with my partners (I'm on the right).

FLORENCE & GARFIELD
BELL GARDENS

CHAPTER 9

City of Commerce & Bell Gardens, 1969

THE EAST L.A. JURISDICTION INCLUDED TWO CONTRACT cities. The City of Commerce was located on the other side of the 5 Freeway from East L.A. and mostly commercial, home to the Sinclair Paint factory and numerous topless bars. Now, it's full of gambling casinos and card clubs but has little blossoming neighborhoods too. The other contract city was Bell Gardens, a little bit farther southeast. It used to be floodplains. Depression-era developers split the farmlands into long, narrow plots with tiny houses sold or rented to families forced from their homes by dust bowls and Manifest Destiny. In 1969, the 2.5 mile area was mostly residential with lots of stores, businesses, and restaurants like Quickie Dog & Taco Quickie and Pioneer Chicken. Factories were just starting to move in to the area.

If I had to assign themes to patrolling in these two cities in 1969, they would be:

Characters are everywhere,
It's all about attitude,
And, respect and responsibility can result in perks.

More Than a Cup of Coffee

My partner, Don Swift—nicknamed Not Too Swift but actually a real sharp guy—and I stopped a driver speeding down the street in Bell Gardens. It turned out that the man owned a famous steakhouse in the area. He had the receipts and proceeds from the night with him and a gun to protect those proceeds. Fortunately for him, it was licensed. My statement to all my partners was simply: "Don't get hurt. We take care of good people, and we arrest bad guys." After assessing that the restaurant owner was a good guy, we let him go, adding, "Slow down!" He was grateful and invited us to his restaurant. "Come on by. I'll give you a cup of coffee."

A couple of nights later, we decided to take him up on it and stopped in, still in uniform because we were on duty. It was a typical steakhouse of that era with dark wood-paneled walls and red tablecloths on the tables. The owner greeted us and told the waitress to give us whatever we wanted.

"So, what do you want?' she asked. "Do you want dinner?"

We went for a cup of coffee, and we left with steaks and potatoes and iced tea. The waitress helped us carry it all out to the police car, along with a red tablecloth that we spread on the hood. We ate in the parking lot where we could keep an eye on the neighborhood. The food was delicious. We returned a couple of times. If you take care of good people, they take care of you.

Helping Us Out

One of the bars we patrolled in Commerce City was called the Chit Chat Bar. We were good friends with the owner, Bobby. He was pro-cop and courteous, so we looked after him and helped him with problems in the bar. In exchange, he would provide us with information about the people and events in the area when needed.

When a deputy was robbed, and the culprit took his gun in the small city of Cudahy across the San Gabriel River, the deputies had no idea who the suspect was. Cudahy was nearby, so I went to Bobby. He had a clue who the suspect was. I got all the information. I submitted a memo to the robbery unit and let them know what I had done to help out this fellow cop. Detectives from that department found him, arrested him, and the deputy's gun was recovered. I never got a thank you or any kind of acknowledgment from the detectives or their department, which was a little annoying, but I certainly thanked Bobby for his help. As I've always seen it, you help out when you can. You thank those that help you. I wish more people acted that way.

Turn Off the Lights

If you're willing to break the rules, there is a price to pay. But if you cooperate, that price doesn't have to be that high. There were plenty of bars in the area, and they were all supposed to close at 2:00 a.m. Driving by one bar in Bell Gardens at about 3:30 in the morning, we found that the parking lot was still full of cars, and we could hear the clinking of glasses and laughter inside. Rather than deal with a lot of drunk people, which could be unpredictable, we walked around to the back, found the electrical breaker on the side of the building, and simply shut off all the power. The bartender came out to see what was wrong with the breaker, and we were there to greet him. We turned the lights back on so customers could see their way out, gave him a ticket for the violation, and called it a night. He didn't give us any problems, so things went smoothly. I'm sure he wasn't happy about the ticket, but he knew it was his own fault.

A Fake Zebra

One of the frequent characters we encountered in Bell Gardens was Theo Franklin Morris, a famous drunk in the area, a big bull of a guy, and he was a frequent problem. Theo owned a burro, not

a horse but a burro, that he spray-painted with black and white stripes to make it look like a zebra. Then he'd go around to the homes in the area and charge money for photographs of little kids on the burro that looked like a zebra. Theo spent most of the money he made either on drugs or on booze at the Chit Chat Bar. When Theo decided to bring the donkey inside with him, Bobby had to kick him out. When Theo and his burro refused to leave, we'd show up to help with their exit.

We were constantly arresting Theo. We arrested him for drug possession numerous times. We once hooked him up for being drunk and disorderly in public. He pleaded not guilty. The case was in Huntington Park Court, the closest judicial court to the arrest. The judge allowed Theo to be his own attorney, which is called pro per. Theo brought a bullwhip to the trial and put it on the table. For whatever reason, the judge allowed this and found him not guilty. He would have gone to jail for a while if he had been found guilty. Instead, he was back on the streets. A few days later, he drove drunk, rear-ended a car, and killed a ten-year-old girl. That girl would be alive if the judge hadn't let him off. Sometimes, letting people off who didn't deserve it had unintended consequences. That little girl and her family paid the price for Theo being back out on the street.

A colleague of mine, J.T., helped us with Theo too. J.T. always tried to make things right. Once he was retired, I visited him at his Sizzler restaurant franchise that he opened on Figueroa Street, near the USC campus. J.T. had a knack for getting to know people and he was well-respected. He introduced me to Mayor Tom Bradley and comedian Redd Foxx's daughter. One Easter Sunday, I took my third wife, Dona, and our son to J.T.'s Sizzler for brunch at his invitation. Things were still pretty segregated then; we were the only white people in the restaurant. People stared at us until J.T. sat down at the table with us. He also insisted on the meal being free, the "police price." He has since passed away, and I miss him a lot. He took care of people, same as me.

Paint Me an Attitude

We weren't the Highway Patrol. I generally didn't give tickets unless I received attitude or saw a good reason. We did pull over guys who would say crap to us like, "Hey, Cop, you're an illegal. You're a bastard." I didn't mind being called a bad name. The work I was doing was important. If someone called me a pig, I'd say, "Sure I'm a pig. Stands for pride, integrity, and guts." I never took offense. People sometimes said bad things to try to get a rise out of us, but I never let it get to me. I never treated anyone disrespectfully when pulling them over. If they were good guys who had made a mistake, I wanted them to learn, but I didn't see why it should cost them any money, especially in a neighborhood where people were barely getting by. However, if they gave me gruff or didn't show any sense of responsibility for their actions, I gave out Attitude Tickets. Of course, that wasn't true of all of my compatriots.

The Sinclair family was still engaged in their family-named paint store chain, which Robert Sinclair opened in the City of Commerce in 1925 with $200 he borrowed from his mother. By the 1960s, under the leadership of Robert Jr., it had become a vast chain throughout California, Nevada, Arizona, and Hawaii. The original City of Commerce store has since closed but was thriving at the time. His son, Robert Sinclair, III, was leaving the store in Commerce in a Lamborghini or a Ferrari (I can't quite remember) going 80 mph in a 30-mph zone. I pulled him over.

"I screwed up," he admitted. He was a good kid. I had some empathy. I had a sports car at the time, my Porsche, so I understood the temptation to drive fast. It was in an area with few people, and he was completely sober.

"Okay," I said, "Don't do that in front of the cops." In this instance, the kid was so touched that I gave him a break that he gave me a painter's discount card for commercial painters. When I painted our house in Manhattan Beach, I got a great price for the paint. And, I never saw him speeding again during my time patrolling the area.

In contrast, having a bad attitude got some guys into trouble. Cruising nights on Whittier Boulevard were every Friday and Saturday nights in those days. The road was bumper to bumper with low riders. My partner, Lopez Tiana, and I joined the line of traffic one night in our patrol car. We hadn't gone far before a young man came towards us, waving his arms to flag us down. He had been shot with a CO2 gun. The pellet had cut through his hair, nicked his earlobe, and creased his neck. He was bleeding but not badly. He was mostly scared.

"Some guys are shooting out store window fronts and stuff," he told us.

"Okay," I said, "get in the back seat. We'll find out who did this to you."

Driving around, scouting the area, we found the culprits pretty quickly. They were young men in a low rider, a '64 Chevy. We instructed the vandals to get out of the car and proceeded to arrest them, but one guy failed the "attitude test." We taught him the error of his ways. He wasn't handled delicately; I'll just leave it at that.

The Ladies Man

I was single and actively dating during this time, still young enough to sow my oats. So, as one does, I ended up dating one-after-the-other three topless entertainers who worked in a bar in the City of Commerce,a strip club that was on my beat. We were there often to keep things in line. Who else did I have time to meet? The first gal was a little crazy. She was quite pretty but had silicone implants that didn't match, one of them noticeably higher than the other. It looked odd, like a grocery bag holding a couple grapefruits. Not the look she was going for. At Christmas, she declared that she wanted a tree. She had a young son whom I never met. So, I went to see a friend who had a Christmas tree lot, bought one, tied the tree on top of the police car, and took it to her house in Montebello. It must've been quite a sight.

The second stripper I just dated two or three times. Not much to say there. The most interesting was the third topless dancer, Stella, a beautiful, sexy woman. She was married but separated, and we went out several times. She told me once, "You know, I've never climaxed in my life." She was about thirty. So, I made helping her achieve this a personal undertaking. I said, "Look, the object is to put the other person first. Think of something that turns you on." It worked the couple of times we went at it. Then I didn't see her again. She probably returned to her husband and said, "Hey, George, here's how you care of your old lady."

I also dated a secretary, a very attractive young lady. I took her to dinner early on to a place called The Cave, which was an atmospheric underground restaurant. We were eating dinner, and she caught me glancing at her cleavage and said, "Eat your dinner so you can keep up your strength."

It was a racy time of my life.

Dangerous Drivers

While dating stripper #3, I had one of my most interesting cases in Bell Gardens which we sometimes called Bell Garbage. Per operating procedure, my partner Dave Kushner, a pleasant and funny guy, and I checked in at the station before our graveyard shift. They had a call for us before we were even in our car. "You've got a drunk driving case with many victims in Bell Gardens." We left the station quickly; the incident was ten minutes away.

When we arrived at the accident scene around 12:30 at night, we saw two cars that had been hit while in motion, multiple parked cars wrecked, and a telephone pole downed along with a mailbox. The driver had even hit a refrigerator for sale on someone's front lawn. It was a total mess. We had at least nine victims, but luckily no injuries. The suspect was gone.

A young girl approached us and said, "If you're looking for the guy, he's around the corner." Sure enough, parked in front of a little house was a car with paint transfer that matched several of the damaged items. We knocked on the door.

The suspect opened it, and we read him his rights. At that time, the charge was 23102, which was drunk driving and a misdemeanor since he hadn't hurt another person's property. But as we were booking him, we saw a closet door open inside the house and a man peeking out at us. When we asked him to come forward, we saw he was injured. He had been a car passenger, making the charge a 23103 felony. The victim also had drugs on him, making him a suspect for possession. We left the scene with two guys in custody and had to write a complex ten-page report. I got good at writing reports; I had to write many of them, some of which were pretty unusual.

Later that shift, at about one in the morning, Dave and I sat at a gas station watching the neighborhood and the Long Beach Freeway while he wrote a report. Suddenly a car drove by going the wrong way on the freeway. We took off after it. A few minutes later, we caught up to the driver, who pulled over when we flashed our lights and siren. It was a woman. Fortunately, she hadn't hit anyone.

She rolled down her window and said, "I'm the Virgin Mary."

"Well, I'm Jesus Christ," I said, "Please get out of the car."

We reported her as a possible 918, an escaped mental patient, got her safely into the back of the squad car and impounded her vehicle. Then we took her to the psychiatric ward at General Hospital, committed as a 5150 WIC for a seventy-two-hour psych evaluation. We may have saved some lives that night. If she had kept driving on the wrong side of the road, she would have surely caused accidents, maybe hit a carload of kids.

Another Day, Another Lost Cop

Officer John Charles Smith of the LAPD had attended my high school a year behind me. We worked together in a paint shop before becoming law enforcement, and he changed his last name from Scott to Smith. I don't know why. John became a motorcycle cop, married a lovely woman named Carol King, and had two kids, a girl and a boy. Given our work together, we had renewed our acquaintance. He was a nice guy.

Officer John Charles Smith

One day, John was parked off the on-ramp to the Pomona freeway, clocking cars with a radar gun and watching for reckless driving. Out of the blue, a drunk driver hit him from behind. John was thrown off his bike, over the railing of the on-ramp, and onto the busy highway, where he was run over many times. I heard about it right away at the station and was shocked and very sad. It happened so quickly, like getting hit by lightning. You never know.

His name is carved into a plaque on the Los Angeles Police Foundation Memorial to Fallen Officers, which used to live at Parker Center in downtown LA when it was the Police Administration Building and is now part of a new brass structure on an elevated plaza in front of the current LAPD headquarters at 100 West 1st Street. His end of watch was March 2, 1966.

Memorial to Fallen Officers in Los Angeles

Family Feuds

Just like in East Los Angeles, we got called to check out a lot of family fights in the contract cities. When the elements of a fight add up to a misdemeanor, you can't arrest the suspects unless you see the fight or someone signs a citizen's complaint. If it's a felony, you don't have to witness it to make an arrest.

Responding to this one family disturbance in Bell Gardens in 1969, we arrived after a guy had punched out his wife. Nine times out of ten, the female victim will later say, either out of fear of complacency, "I don't want to sign a complaint." But this woman signed a complaint on the guy, and we cuffed him for wife beating and took him to the station, but this man was angry. He was so hot that he broke my pen on the aluminum counter after signing the booking slip. I added a charge of malicious mischief for breaking my pen, which meant he had to pay me back for the damage. It was a good Cross pen.

***

We were always getting calls from this one couple in Bell Gardens, not married but dating, that were always fighting. Both of them had the IQ of a pencil. They called us once because the woman had fallen and split her head open. Blood had dried in her hair by the time we got there. We just told her to go to the hospital. Another time, they called us not for a fight or an injury but because they wanted to get married. My partner and I looked at each other, amused.

"Okay," I said. I took out my book of penal codes and my badge to make it look official. I had no power to marry them, but they didn't know that. They stood together in front of me while their two little dogs fornicated between us. "Alright, you're married," I said, "But it's only good for three days." The guy took a paper cigar band off a Roi-Tan cigar and put it on her finger as a wedding ring. It was comical, but I guess it calmed the waters. We never heard from those two again.

***

If marriage can make people crazy; divorce is much worse. One night, we got a call about a disturbance in a trailer park in Bell Gardens. It was another 918, the code for "Insane Person." When we arrived, this woman—I can't make this up—had a chainsaw and was trying to cut her trailer in half.

I asked her, "Excuse me, Ma'am. What are you doing?"

"We're getting a divorce. The judge said we have to cut everything in half."

There were good times, bad times, and strange times while working nights in Los Angeles. Chainsaws were a bit much.

***

Sometimes we just had to blow off some steam. I was patrolling with another partner on an unusually slow night when we passed John Ford Park Lake. "Stop," said my partner, "I'm going to get a duck." In the winter, the little commercial lake in Bell Gardens attracted many migrating ducks flying south from Oregon and Washington. They came to Southern California for the warmer weather.

It was about 1:00 in the morning. The only weapon we had was a 12-gauge shotgun with a short barrel. My partner said, "Okay, Bob, you go scare them out." He took a double-aught buck with just a few .33 caliber pellets and put bird-shot in it. I drove to the lake's other end and turned on the headlights. Ducks flew over his head. He shot—*bam!*—and bagged a bird. We went to an all-night laundromat where he rolled up his sleeves and plucked the feathers. After his shift, he cooked it up at home. That was a memorable shift.

On Foot Patrol on Catalina Island

I did a few patrolling stints on Catalina Island and that was always a nice change of pace. The L.A. County Sheriff's Department was contracted to police the rocky island of Catalina, located in the Pacific, 28 miles south of Long Beach. Its history is similar to the rest of California, with its native population displaced after the arrival of Spanish and Franciscan friars. It became a Mexican land grant purchased by wealthy American real estate investors, who turned it from a cattle ranch into a resort destination, creating the main town of Avalon. Chewing gum magnate William

Me in plain clothes on Catalina Island.

Wrigley Jr. invested millions in new infrastructure and attractions in the 1920s, including the Catalina Casino and Ballroom. Since he owned the Chicago Cubs, the island became the location of their spring training. Philip K. Wrigley, William's son, was the main honcho when I was there in 1970. He maintained the island until he deeded it in 1975 to the Catalina Conservancy Society, which he had established.

At that time, Catalina had a population of about 1,500, plus the continual waves of tourists. In addition to a nine-hole golf course and an impressive mausoleum on the hill where old man Wrigley was buried, the island had a small airport ten miles from town on a plateau on the highest part of the island. It was

That's me on the right on Catalina, clearly enjoying the assignment.

frightening to land there or take off from the "Airport in the Sky." That was what the locals called it because the runway ended with a steep drop-off on either side. P. K. Wrigley had a beautiful, refurbished DC-3 from World War II parked in a garage up there, a C-47, they called it, painted red, white, and blue, in perfect condition. I admired that.

Wrigley and his family spent a lot of time on the island, as did many vacationing celebrities. A few other notable people lived on the island, such as Western author Zane Grey, who had a house on the hill overlooking Avalon. On the rest of the island were cattle, sheep, feral goats, and feral pigs. Most of these animals have since been cleared by the Conservancy, leaving the grazing land to an American bison herd established there in the late 1920s when several were brought onto the island for a movie shoot.

They used to have a small police department on the island, but it had been defunct for a while, and their old building became our headquarters. Some deputies who arrived there before me got a little liquid courage at a local bar and threw a rock through the glass window that read Catalina Police, declaring, "This is part of the Sheriff's Department now." By the time I got there, the window had been replaced and read "Los Angeles Sheriff's Department."

Catalina was a good assignment, quite the contrast to East L.A. My first assignment on the island was for a week with my partner, Ralph Simmons. No cars are allowed on the island, just shuttles to move people around and a few jeeps. So, our job was to walk around Avalon and watch people, keeping an eye on things. We had no boss there to report to, and we didn't have any trouble all week, so it was pretty nice.

During our off-hours, we took a jeep to the other side of the island toward Twin Harbors, where actress Natalie Wood drowned in 1981. We stopped at Shark Harbor and went free diving with pry bars to pop abalone off the rocks. We had to be careful because abalone is the favorite food of moray eels, and we didn't want to attract them. Once back in the kitchen of the place we were staying, we beat and breaded the abalone meat with a rubber mallet and fixed them up. They were delicious.

Another time, Don Dunlop and I were assigned to Catalina Island for Labor Day. It was a big party weekend on the island. We were eating out with a couple of young ladies during our off-hours when Deputy Ron Ablott entered the restaurant in his uniform. An excellent officer, he had a photographic memory which served him well. He later retired from arson and explosives, both very dangerous jobs. He said, "Hey, we want you guys to down a door. They're doing drugs inside." We excused ourselves from our dates, followed Ron to the house, kicked in the door, and made the arrest. Don and I went back and finished our meal with the ladies. That was fun.

CHAPTER 10

SWAT: Special Enforcement Bureau, 1969-1971

I
N 1969, I WAS EXCITED TO LEAVE EAST L. A. to join the SWAT team. I wanted to work SWAT because they're the elite, the best of the best, and I figured there'd be no problems with anybody I was working with. To be on the SWAT team, we couldn't have any baggage in our backgrounds and had to have a level head with no instances of brutality. We also had to be able to write strong reports, be on time, and not be a problem. I was pleased to be accepted into the program.

Shooting on the range in SWAT training

As I started this new chapter in my career, I moved to an apartment in Manhattan Beach with Deputy Al Chancellor. Life was good there. We were two bachelors living near the beach, and we both had Porsches. His was a 1965 Porsche 356, and I had my 1969 Porsche 912. Al met his first wife while we lived there, and I met my second wife—a short marriage—and then my wonderful third wife.

Al passed away from Alzheimer's just before this book was written. He was an exceptional person. We were very like-minded in our focus on helping others through our work. Our apartment in Manhattan Beach was a great place to come home to after some of the work we did, especially during the two-and-a-half years I was on the SWAT team.

SWAT stands for Special Weapons and Tactics. To be on the team, I had to go through a special training at the Camp Pendleton Marine base, where we stayed in Little Vietnam Village, which was named that because it housed over 1,000 Southeast Asian refugees

A squadmate repelling at Camp Pendleton

during and just after the Vietnam War. Though the training at Camp Pendleton was only for two days, we learned a great deal there.

We rappelled off buildings, and some guys even did it out of helicopters. We sharpened our shooting skills at the range with more powerful weapons than we had used previously on the job. We learned advanced first aid and tactical strategies. We learned how to deal with barricaded suspects, hostage situations, riots, undercover operations, remote emergency situations, high-risk search and seizure operations and more. Whenever a suspect grabbed us by the neck or put a gun to our head, we were instructed to drop to the ground so the culprit would be left vulnerable and exposed. I'm happy to report that I excelled at the training. It was great.

It was an impressive group of eighty men, but we were nothing like the SWAT teams of today. The L.A. Sheriff's SWAT team when this book was written was rumored to be the best in the country. These days, the Navy Seals train them, and their weapons are much more advanced than ours were. They practice with MP5 submachine guns, full automatics, and Benelli shotguns. Our SWAT team used an earlier version of the Benelli shotgun. It was an automatic 12-gauge shotgun that could fire eight rounds before the first casing hit the ground.

We took the quick-kill course, which I still practice on the range when I go. It is a tactical system the military developed. You don't stand up to aim and shoot. You squat down and look over the top of the gun, not worrying about perfect aim, and fire your first round for effect. You can get six shots off before the guy who's checking his aim even fires one. My partner got hurt practicing quick-kill. He fell off a roof and injured his back at Pendleton. Training for SWAT duty was dangerous.

We shot AT4s, an anti-tank weapon, nicknamed eighty-four or just The Law. It's a one-shot, Swedish 84 mm (3.31 in) unguided, man-portable, disposable, shoulder-fired recoilless device. You shoot it once and throw it away, but the explosion will take out a tank. We also fired a grenade launcher. It was humbling. And pretty cool.

They showed us how dangerous ammonium nitrate was. That was the same substance that Timothy McVeigh would use in the Oklahoma City bombing in 1995. Our instructors had a small sack of it. They put some fuel in the sack and added a dynamite cap. We were three hundred yards away when they lit the fuse. The explosion was huge.

We also learned to work with C-4, a moldable explosive that looks like white chocolate and can be shaped and pressed like Silly Putty. You can put it around doorways to blow open a door. With a dynamite cap in it, it can take out a wall. It was all so exciting.

When they fed us lunch at Camp Pendleton, they gave us each a box of K-rations from World War II, a meal prepared twenty-five years earlier. The box contained a can of beef stew or spaghetti, Chiclets gum, and three Lucky Strike cigarettes. Some of the guys smoked them. The cigarettes were so old and dry that after two puffs, there was nothing left. They showed us how to heat the can of stew by cutting off a small piece of C-4, putting it under the can, and lighting it with a match to act as a Bunsen burner. However, you had to be careful. It could blow an arm off if you didn't put a dynamite cap on it.

Nobody complained about the K-rations. When you were on the SWAT team, you did whatever you were told, no matter what it was. We had all volunteered for this program and wanted to be there. There was no sniveling or complaining. It was like being in the military. If the sergeant said, "Take that hill," we took that hill. If a trainee said, "I'm afraid of heights," the response he would get most likely is: "Bullshit, get your ass up there!" That's the way it was. I successfully completed training, and my SWAT duties began.

We had two different special force groups within the SWAT team: Emergency Services Detail (ESD) and the Special Enforcement Bureau (SEB). The ESD was part of the Special Weapons team. Those guys formed the Mountain Rescue Team and the Ocean Rescue Team. Mountain Rescue rappelled into a thick forest. Ocean Rescue trained in deep sea diving with the famous Jacques Cousteau in the dive tank at UCLA, using a combination of gases in their scuba tanks to go into very deep water. Both teams did all kinds of other superhero stunts.

I was a part of the other special ops group, the Special Enforcement Bureau (SEB). We handled high-risk tactical operations involving barricaded suspects, hostage situations, and high-risk warrant services. The SEB also provided security for visiting dignitaries and politicians, including the President and Vice-President of the United States. The SEB often worked together as four-man teams. One man was a sniper—that was me, I had a .308 rifle. Another teammate had an AR-15, another had teargas, and the last was the medic, who carried a .45. The ESD and SEB often worked together on missions.

The SWAT guys were all true professionals, as I had hoped they would be, great to work with. Even with eighty guys in the unit, in the two-and-a-half years I was in the SEB, we never had anyone lose it or get caught up in a brutality beef. We went to the worst situations—riots, major drug busts, stake outs, and to apprehend murderers—and we had only one shooting, which would later be called the Newhall Massacre.

During my time on SWAT, the only person I knew who was killed was a former partner, Larrell Smith, in 1983. We were serving a warrant against a drug dealer, and he shot Larrell as the deputy was making an entry through the front window. Our team opened fire and killed the suspect.

Los Angeles Sheriff's SWAT team, 1969.

Looking for a Lost Hiker

While the ESD and SEB mostly operated as separate units in SWAT, we worked together on a mission in the San Gabriel Mountains soon after completing our training, looking for a lost hiker. We stayed overnight in our mobile command post, a modified Beaver Coach bus called a 3-Henry that contained restrooms, sleeping facilities, weapons, ammunition, and communications equipment. We traveled in that vehicle to respond to various emergencies like wildfires, earthquakes, and rescues. Once in the mountains, we followed our commands from leadership and searched in teams in different areas. We combed the area but couldn't find the missing hiker. It was approaching 1300 hours, and we had already been in the woods for nearly twelve hours. Sometimes, missions like these could go on for as long as thirty-six hours.

The sergeant, a two-striper senior deputy like me, said, "Let's go, 98." Code 98 meant: Wrap it up and go home.

"Hey, Sarge, let's give it another half hour," I suggested,

"because if we go 98, pack it in, the rescue guys will come down from the mountains. They have rescue gear that they have deployed. Let's just wait thirty minutes." About fifteen minutes later, they found him. Had we wrapped it up, the guy would have died. I felt good about that call.

Members of my team in front of the mobile unit.

Foot Patrol

There was uniform duty and non-uniform duty when working SWAT. When working uniformed SWAT, we didn't have the same duties as regular officers but instead assisted the regular station deputies on their calls, and we were also called in as a presence to cut down on crime. To this end, we did many foot patrols in high-crime areas like Hollywood and some of the rougher neighborhoods. I often worked with my SWAT teammate, Don Dunlop. He was born in England, and he was an ex-movie stuntman. He knew martial arts and looked like Crocodile

Dundee. Dunlop introduced me to Joe Gold, the bodybuilder, weightlifter, and founder of Gold's Gym in Venice. Dunlop knew Arnold Schwarzenegger, too. They were all part of a bodybuilding community.

One warm night with the Santa Ana winds blowing, Don and I were in front of the Classy Cat strip club on foot patrol. Nearby, we saw a man in a London Fog overcoat, which was odd because it was too heavy for the warm weather. He was acting suspiciously, so we watched him for a while. He was flashing people, opening his coat to women. When we approached him, we found he had cut a hole in his trousers, exposing his private parts. We took him behind the Classy Cat and very severely told him of the error of his ways. We didn't have to take a report. That was enough to straighten him up, and we never saw him again. We used to call that Curbside Justice or Taking Care of Business, otherwise known as TCB. It was often more effective than booking someone and taking him to jail.

While on foot patrol, I made it a habit to converse with teenagers on the streets whenever I saw them. Mostly 15- to 17-year-olds, these kids often talked about quitting school. "Listen," I said, "If you quit school, you'll have no diploma, no skills. Do you know what kind of jobs you can get? How little you'll get paid? And that you will likely be the last hired and first fired from any job? You're not going to be performing surgery. What kind of girls are you going to get, huh? Stay in school, learn a trade, get your education." I used myself as an example. "I don't have a college degree, but I got my act together and did this. I had to. And I like it and make decent money. Find something you like, and you'll excel at it if you like it and work at it." Who knows if they listened, but I had to try.

We tried to treat the prostitutes with respect as we talked to them and checked out their situations for abuse or any leads on other crimes. One day, I told a group of women, "Look, if you keep doing this, what will it be like for you in ten days? How about a year? Five years? You're on a road to nowhere." I don't think they listened, and I'm sure some of them felt stuck in their current lives, but I tried to give them a different perspective.

While keeping an eye on the neighborhoods and spending a lot of time teaching people how to behave in Hollywood, it wasn't unusual to spot a famous star. One night, we saw basketball player Wilt Chamberlain from across the street as he entered the Whiskey a Go Go, a historic nightclub on the Sunset Strip. You couldn't miss him with his height. Since we were in uniform, he waved, and I went over to talk to him. People gathered around, but he wasn't bothered by it at all. He seemed like a good dude.

Afterward, I returned to our black and white, parked around the corner on Wilshire Boulevard. My partner, Ed Purpercy, had a man in custody. The guy was so loaded he was sitting on the fender of our police car, trying to sell us secobarbital, pills also called Reds or Red Devils on the street. As we read him his rights, he resisted arrest. He didn't want to go to jail. There was a little altercation, and he pushed Ed against a plate glass window of a storefront. Fortunately, the window didn't break, but the suspect just upped his sentence. We hooked the man up for the sale of drugs and resisting arrest.

We took him to the station and booked him. On the way, Ed realized his badge was gone. It had fallen off his shirt during the struggle. Once the perpetrator was processed, we went back to where we made the arrest and started combing the ground with flashlights. We were approached by a hippie in jeans and boots with long hair and a backpack. I wasn't keen on hippies then, but this young man had found the badge and wanted to return it to us. That taught me a lesson: Never judge someone by their looks. It's about character, about deeds. That's what makes someone who they are. How they dress or talk or walk or wear their hair, the color of their skin—none of those things matter. They don't determine the quality of a person.

Honesty seemed to be a rare commodity in daily police life. Suspicion was part of the job. You had to use observation, questions, and instincts when dealing with suspects. I had a friend who worked in the technical section of the Sheriff's Department administering lie detector tests. He told me how to beat the machine. I won't reveal what he said because I don't want people to use the method, but those tests couldn't always show who was telling the truth. It could be tricky, like in the case of the candy red Chevy.

The Candy Red '55 Chevy

One day, we were transporting some equipment in a radio car for the annual Hay Festival in Lancaster. I was a passenger in the squad car that day when Homicide contacted us on the radio. "We're looking for a candy red '55 Chevy with bullet hubcaps. The suspect is a Latino with body tattoos and wearing a beanie."

I knew exactly what a '55 series Chevy looked like because I used to have one. We made a U-turn and went down San Fernando Road toward the area where the homicide occurred on Kagel Canyon Road, northeast of San Fernando Valley. We saw it heading the other way on the road—a '55 Chevy, candy apple red, driven by a guy with a beanie and tats. We wheeled around and tried to stop him. He didn't stop. We could see him moving around inside the car. It looked like he was stuffing something under his seat or pulling something out. We had to assume he might be arming himself, so when we pulled up in the lane next to him, I pointed my gun at him out the window. That got him to pull over.

At gunpoint now, we had him step out of the car, cuffed him, read him his rights, searched him, and put him in the back of our car, proceeding with caution the entire time because he was a homicide suspect. We searched his vehicle and saw what he had been stuffing under his seat: one hundred and fifty balloons of heroin. And, it turned out, he was on parole.

What had been reported to the police was that this guy had stopped his red Chevy on Kagel Canyon where a man and his wife were having car trouble. The suspect pulled out a knife and killed the wife. But the story didn't feel right. We had arrested this guy and spent time with him while booking him. The drug charges were secure enough, but the stabbing didn't ring true, and he denied it.

Sure enough, the accusation turned out to be bogus. When Homicide investigates murders, they check if anyone has recently increased the insurance policy on a spouse, parent, or child. The husband had upped the insurance policy on his wife. They brought him in and got a confession out of him. He had murdered his wife; our suspect wasn't even there. The husband happened to see our suspect drive by in his red Chevy and had concocted the whole story. They both went to prison—the man for killing his wife and our original suspect for possession of heroin and parole violation.

Sweet Dicky

My partner, Dicky Madden, or "Sweet Dicky," was an amazing guy, full of character and the funniest person I knew. He was my best man at my second wedding. We worked together at the Rose Bowl when I once again was there in 1969. Being in SEB, we had much bigger security roles. Dicky and I were assigned to ring the goalposts in the end zone after the football game to stop people from breaking them and taking home bits as souvenirs. At the time, they were made of wood, and people would knock them down, break a piece off, take it home, and put the shard on their mantels.

Just before the game ended, we stood near the end zone ready to take our places when the game ball was kicked. After hitting the ground, it rolled over to Dick who picked it up. The referee said, "Give me the ball." He put his arms out like, *Throw it over here.* Dick turned around and threw the ball into the stands like football players do when they score. Then he did this great flex like bodybuilders do in competitions because he was a bodybuilder himself. The crowd cheered. They loved him. It was funnier than hell.

*Dick Madden admiring his reflection,
Isla Vista, 1970*

We were constantly in and out of the bars and clubs in Hollywood, looking for illegal activity, including drag clubs and gay bars. At the gay bars, if Dick saw some guys that looked suspicious, he would cut in for a dance and chat them up. Once, we stopped this guy in drag who we suspected of possession. We had to search him for drugs and guns and had him up against the side of the patrol car with his dress over his head, exposing his undergarments. It was quite a sight but, believe it or not, it was good for him and his family. It turned out that he was the son of a very high public official. With his skirt over his head, people couldn't see his face while we made the arrest. We hooked him up for drugs, but nothing more than that.

It was always a good time with Dicky Madden. He and I were very close. Everyone in SEB knew that they might get pranked by Dicky at any time. And nothing was sacred! More than once I heard Dicky say to another deputy in the showers, "Hey, George, you've got the most beautiful Johnson I've ever seen in my life. You ought to be proud of that." The guys got mad or embarrassed that Dicky was complementing their penises. Or he sometimes pinched them on the ass, just to get a rise out them. One time he stood on a chair above the showers and added a little "golden shower" for one of our colleagues. These kinds of pranks were part of the office culture. We needed some levity in our lives as cops.

140

Luckily Dick could take it as well as dish it out. He drove a little sports car, an Austin Healey. One time in 1969 while we were on duty, a bunch of the guys in the office—also recipients of his tricks and jokes—muscled his car into the locker room and placed it on top of the benches. When we got back from patrol duty, there it was. It was quite a sight!

Dick Madden's car in the SEB locker room

Dicky and I were stopped for coffee one day while on patrol in Hollywood. The LAPD Hollywood division was next to our West Hollywood Sheriff's station, and we met with some of their deputies. There were four of us—the LAPD guys in their blues, and us in our tan and green uniforms. They had a captain they didn't like. In fact, they hated him. So, to play a trick on him, they put his name and home phone number in a personal ad in a gay magazine. The ad read, "Financially secure 45-year-old male looking for a new adventure." The captain never found out who did it. I never did anything like that, but those boys in the LAPD sure did.

I did play a prank on Don Scott, another of my partners for a time. He liked to vacation in Chicago, taking his girlfriend and leaving his wife at home. He always flew United Airlines. I called him one day and said, "Mr. Scott, this is Mr. Collins from United Airlines." That was my undercover name, Wayne Collins. I said, "You're going to Chicago. We've got to take the armrests out to fit your backside in the seat, and we'll have to charge you double."

He got quiet for a few seconds. Then he said, "Bobby, that's you!" Don and I always played a lot of tricks on each other.

Tailing an Old Gangster

The SWAT team did surveillance on some heavy hitters. One of them had been a member of the old Detroit Purple Gang. While Al Capone's gang shook up Chicago in the 1930s, the Purple Gang had reigned in Detroit. Bootlegging, bookmaking, prostitution, murders, scams—the Purple Gang was involved in all of it. During Prohibition, they were known for bringing in liquor on speedboats from Toronto, Canada, to Detroit.

By 1970, this gangster was an elderly man, around 80. He had "retired" to Studio City, a high-end area in the hills overlooking San Fernando Valley. We didn't know how involved he still was in criminal activity, so we regularly conducted helicopter surveillance on his house to keep track of his movements. This one day, the guys in the air radioed that he had pulled out of his garage in his Rolls Royce and was on the move. We tailed him in undercover cars over the hill into West Hollywood, where he entered a large mansion. We were informed that the house belonged to the vice president of a professional sports team in L.A. There was a concern that this guy might be trying to fix games.

There was no violence that day, no arrests made, and I don't know if there was tampering with games or what happened after that. It was often the case doing my job that I wouldn't find out the end of a story. I just had to do my part to report on the action. Still, I found it fascinating, you know, that this guy had been an OC most of his life and was still at large. And the possibility was real that big bets and pay-offs might be affecting the outcome of major professional sports.

Working the Academy Awards

A fun SWAT assignment was the annual task of working security for the Academy Awards. I was there for the Oscar ceremonies in 1969 and 1970. It was great. At that time, the

142

ceremony was held in the Dorothy Chandler Pavilion near the Hall of Justice. The reason why LASD had security duty instead of the police department was because it was a county building, not city.

Deputies with seniority worked inside with a gun hidden under their tuxedos. The guys with less seniority worked outside in uniform. I had seniority at that point and worked inside, dressed to the nines. Despite our suits, however, it was clear who we were. A lot of the actors and actresses didn't like us, of course.

Actress Martha Raye, who was honored at the 1969 Oscars, was an exception. Staying true to her nickname, The Big Mouth, she held up her hands when she walked by me and yelled, "Search me!" and gave me a big mischievous smile. Katherine Hepburn won the award for Best Actress that year.

SEB security with John Wayne at the Academy Awards, 1973

It was a fun duty. I didn't care much about famous people, although some of my colleagues were excited to take a picture with John Wayne when he won his first and only Oscar in 1970 for Best Actor. I just like to be around good people. I don't have much time for phonies

Beach Patrol

One day, we were assigned to check out Zuma Beach near the Orange County line in plain clothes and in our own cars. There had been a rash of car burglaries there. We made our presence known and did some debriefing. Then we "debriefed" in a different way and went swimming. Why not? We changed into swimsuits in our cars and took a quick dip. You take a perk when you can get it.

Not long after, we had a lot of fun off-duty swimming in Cross Creek, which ran behind the Malibu Station. A bunch of us on the SWAT team hiked up the canyon to a great swimming hole with a rope swing. A few guys pretended like they were Tarzan and splashed into the stream. Some of the deputies caught a rattlesnake, butchered it, and barbecued it, washing it down with beers. This camaraderie increased the loyalty we felt for each other. Each of us knew we would die for our partners if it came down to it. Among some, this went as far as a little vigilante justice. "If some cockroach kills me, he doesn't go to court," someone might say. Everyone knew what that meant. Luckily, I never faced that dilemma.

Profiling and Hostage Negotiations

One night, I was working in South L.A. with Don Swift. There had been a lot of robberies in the area. To put it plainly, when we scanned the streets, we did profile people, but for me, at least, it wasn't racial profiling like people think of today. It was about spotting unusual and suspicious behavior, actions, or characteristics that didn't fit the situation. Sometimes, it turned out to be simply unusual behavior.

This happened when we ID-ed a man walking down the street holding a plastic jug. It didn't look right. The jug was full of gasoline. You could smell it. He was also carrying some blue paper towels from the gas station. Once we talked to him and asked him a few questions, I realized he was okay, but I thought I'd joke around with him a little since he didn't seem like the sharpest knife in the drawer. "I'm going to arrest you for having a Molotov cocktail," I said.

He looked at me like I was crazy, "Man, I ain't got no moderate cocktail."

More often than not, profiling led to a suspect in a crime. For example, on the street, if I saw a guy with a big bulge in his pocket, maybe looking around furtively, I would approach him, suspecting he might have a gun or drugs. If I saw a sixteen-year-old kid driving a Ferrari, I'd wonder: Did he steal it?

That same night, we pulled over a suspicious-looking Chevy Camaro. When we approached the car, we saw that this guy had no seats in it. He was sitting on a plastic milk crate to drive. Cockroaches were running around the interior. When we questioned him, we learned that he had sold the car seats for drugs. I'd never seen that before.

And yes, back then, if we saw a white guy in an all-black neighborhood, we might question him. Chances were that he was there to buy drugs or do something else illegal. As we questioned people, I was always respectful. I might say, "What are you doing? What's going on, Man?" It was simply about talking to people. We never profiled a particular person based on race alone. I don't care about the color of people's skin. It was always about what the person was doing and if it didn't fit the situation. When an area experienced increased crime, we'd just talk to people, ask around, and let them know we were there.

However, we did fill in FIR cards for any suspicious person. FIR stands for Field Investigative Report. The report included the person's name, address, features like hair and skin color, height, build, and any tattoos or piercings. We held on to the FIR cards. If someone later said, "Hey, this guy robbed me. He had a skull on his arm," we'd go back through the cards to see if anyone matched that description. It was just good police work.

Another day with Don, a car passed us going fast. The back end was weighed down so much that it almost scraped the asphalt. It could've been bad shocks. He also could have stolen an ATM or had a safe in his trunk.

"That's a good shake. Let's go stop him," said Don. We followed him up and down streets as he increased his speed. He was definitely up to something. His car was faster than our squad car, but we were able to stay on his tail until we hit two bumps in the road. We hit the second one so hard that it tore the oil pan off the underside of our car. The chase was over. We sat and waited for a tow truck to pull us back to the station. Don had to write a report on the damage to a county vehicle.

In this job, you win some and you lose some. I remember when the SWAT team won a big one, thanks to Bill Baker., our hostage negotiator. This case made the front page of the *L.A. Times*. There was a robbery at a jewelry store in Marina Del Rey, a botched robbery. The suspects didn't get away before the police were on the scene, but the employees of the store were in there with the perpetrators, held at gunpoint. That's when they brought Bill in. But the hostage negotiations were not going well. That's when Bill did something we were never trained to do. Following his gut, he took off his shirt, raised his arms so the suspects could see he wasn't armed, and backed into the store. He explained to the robbers that he was just there to talk, that if they hurt him in any way the rest of the cops would open fire and kill them. Then he convinced the robbers inside that there wasn't a way out. He gave it a few moments for the news to sink in. They believed him and surrendered. It's true;

if they had done any harm to Bill, the cops would have probably killed them. He explained to me later that it helped that he was Black, as were the suspects. Based on the situation, he felt he could gain their trust. With his experience and intuition, Bill was able to save the hostages before anyone got hurt and apprehend the suspects peacefully. It's no wonder that he later became a commander.

Dealing with Hells Angels

My work in the SEB got really serious when we had to deal with gang activity. Southern California had a lot of biker gangs in the late 1960s and 1970s. The big ones were the Gypsy Jokers, the Coffin Cheaters, and the infamous Hells Angels. The Coffin Cheaters no longer exist, although Australia and Norway both have biker gangs of the same name. The Hells Angels are still the best known today. The gang originated on March 17, 1948, in Fontana, California, when several small, rebellious motorcycle clubs agreed to merge. When I knew them as a deputy, they were involved in multiple criminal activities, including armed robbery, arson, assault, counterfeiting, drug trafficking, fraud, gunrunning, homicide, identity theft, and prostitution.

Today, not every chapter is involved in crime. However, they're still categorized as "outlaw" motorcycle clubs because they are not sanctioned by the American Motorcyclist Association (AMA) and do not adhere to the AMA's rules. Instead, the clubs have their own bylaws that reflect outlaw biker culture. The U.S. Department of Justice defines "outlaw motorcycle gangs" as "organizations whose members use their motorcycle clubs as conduits for criminal enterprises."

When I patrolled in Norwalk, we often were called to the Holiday Bar, where the bikers hung out. When I was on SWAT, a couple of deputies I knew responded to break up a fight at the bar. One of the officers was a tough guy, and while breaking up the disturbance, he destroyed these two bikers that became

147

violent with him. According to the story I heard, one suspect had a broken arm, and the other guy had a broken leg. I was in court waiting on another case when I saw that these bikers were being tried, so I popped into the courtroom. The attorney defending the two suspects in this Holiday Bar situation told the judge, "Your Honor, I'd like a psych evaluation on the deputy involved. He was an animal. He broke my defendants' arm and leg." But the judge denied the request. From the deputy's point of view, he was just TCB—taking care of business. In the department, it was also sometimes called an "Attitude Adjustment."

While I was on SWAT, the Hells Angels were having a wake for a fallen member in El Monte. Neighbors complained of loud music, shots fired, and other disturbances. We got the call to respond because the clubs tended to be armed and aggressive. Even in those days, Hells Angels were the feared outlaw motorcycle club, so we approached with ten two-man cars as we drove from Hollywood to El Monte. According to San Diego PD intelligence, who kept watch over the burial in San Diego, the Hells Angels had urinated on the casket of the deceased as part of their memorial, a strange ritual.

The wake in El Monte after the burial was at a residential home. Our sergeant, Reggie Lawson, went to the door cautiously while we backed him up, since we knew they had guns. He told them to cease and desist. They didn't like that. They threw a motorcycle chain at him. He ducked and the chain hit a radio car, putting dents in it. We backed off.

Their reaction made it a more dangerous situation, a 245, Assault with a Deadly Weapon, so changed tactics. Reggie had another deputy and me get on the roof of the building across the street as lookouts. Every time someone came out the front door, we radioed the men on the ground, and they pursued, stopped, and arrested each one, usually for carrying weapons on their motorcycles or in their cars or for drunk driving. Whenever a man came out of the house, he never returned.

After a while, we were replaced on the roof. It was our turn to take prisoners. With my partner driving, we pulled over a guy in his car soon after he left the wake. I put a gun to his face through the open driver's side window so he knew it was serious. He failed the sobriety test and had a gun in the car. We hooked him up, and he plead guilty, resulting in twenty days in jail.

Back at the house, the Hells Angels group woke up to what was happening. One called the Temple City Sheriff's station and complained, "Hey, everyone that leaves never comes back."

After that, the rest of them gave up. At Temple Station, officers confiscated the bikers' leather jackets and vests, identifying them as Hells Angels. Each was covered with patches, including the required patch that read "One Percenter." In the 1960s, the AMA tried to distance itself from the Hells Angels, saying they represented only "one percent of the motorcycle-riding public." Many clubs seized on the one-percenter label as a badge of honor and a way to mock the establishment. The deputies at Temple Station bleached all the Hells Angels colors, the red and white patches on their jackets, in the washing machine.

Appropriated Hells Angel flags on display

In the California Police Olympics

It was a good thing that with all that SWAT training, I was probably in the best shape of my life. One summer day at the SEB headquarters, the guys starting a shift were all in the locker room getting ready for foot patrol when the sergeant approached me.

"Hey, did you ever swim, Bob? Like competitively?"

"I haven't swum since high school," I told him, "Why?"

It was time for the 1970 Police Olympics, in which all the various law enforcement agencies in California competed against each other in traditional Olympic sports. A San Diego policeman named Veon "Duke" Nyhus and a few like-minded colleagues began the annual event in 1967. Duke created the competition to promote physical fitness and sport for officers to improve their overall fitness, reduce stress, and to increase their professional abilities. It was a great idea.

Evidently our LASD swimming relay team was missing a swimmer. I told them I couldn't promise them anything, least of all a victory, but hey, why not? I'm in.

The annual event was headquartered in Tahoe, but the event took place in Reno, Nevada, that year. I was given time off duty that Thursday through Sunday to participate. Everyone was bringing girlfriends and wives. Being single at the time, I brought a gal I was dating from Costa Mesa. There were teams from cities all over the state there, representing the Highway Patrol, police departments, other sheriff departments, county Marshal departments. Even the California-based FBI had a team. It was very fun. In the evenings after the competitions, many adult beverages were consumed. There was a lot of laughter and storytelling. As an added bit of irony, a bank was robbed while we were all there, hundreds of officers of the various law enforcement branches. If the thieves had only known! The local police force took care of it, so we didn't find out about it until later.

As for our relay race, I swam the first leg. A guy in LAPD

dusted me! It was the only time I participated in the California Police Olympics. It has since grown into a nation-wide event drawing thousands of athletes representing Law Enforcement, Firefighter, Emergency Medical Technicians, Customs, and Correctional Officers as well as full time employees (active or retired) of any eligible

agency. As for Duke, he lived to be 84 years old, a rare old-timer, retired officer like me. Good, positive living—it makes a difference.

Yours Truly at the California Police Olympics, 1970

CHAPTER 11

The Newhall Massacre, 1970

PEOPLE WHO LIVED IN LOS ANGELES at the time know about the Newhall Incident or Massacre of 1970. It was in all the newspapers and on all the news programs on TV. Our SWAT team was there on the scene.

Alerted to two armed suspects in a Pontiac Grand Prix, two young CHP officers, Roger Gore and Walt Frago, spotted the vehicle in question on the highway and followed them down an offramp in Valencia near Magic Mountain amusement park and into the parking lot of a coffee shop. The two policemen made a huge tactical error, perhaps because they were only 23 years old and had been on the force for less than two years, or perhaps they just miscalculated the risk. As highway patrol officers, they weren't trained for felony arrests; they were trained to oversee traffic.

The driver, a 27-year-old ex-felon named Bobby Davis, initially cooperated with the officers, stepping out of the car when Officer Gore told him to do so. Gore proceeded to search him. Officer Frago approached the other side of the car where Jack Twining, also an ex-con, was sitting in the passenger seat. Frago carried his shotgun at port arms, with the stock against his hip and the barrel pointed in the air. Seeing this, Twining exited the car, opened fire with a Smith & Wesson Model 28 revolver, and killed Frago with two rounds before the officer could even aim his weapon. Officer

Gore drew his Colt Python and returned fire, losing focus on Davis, who pulled a .38 Special out of his waistband and killed Gore with two shots at point-blank range.

The officers' backup, two more CHPs, arrived on the scene. The criminals immediately opened fire on them, diving back into the Pontiac for more weapons. The ex-felons were planning a bank robbery and had amassed twice the number of weapons as the four CHP officers. The shoot-out continued until both of the backup officers, George Alleyn and James Pence, 24 years old, were also killed.

While the shoot-out was raging, a 31-year-old former U.S. Marine ran in to drag one of the officers to safety. Unable to keep going under fire, he grabbed the officer's pistol

Fallen officers, husbands, fathers

and fired back, hitting the Pontiac and Davis but not enough to incapacitate him. The assisting citizen was finally forced to take cover in a ditch. After the exchange of gunfire, the two killers fled through the darkness, each in separate directions, taking the officers' firearms with them and leaving behind four dead cops. All four were married and had a combined total of seven children, now fatherless.

That's when we were called to the scene. It was close to three in the morning when we were ordered to look for these guys. Our SEB team divided up in pursuit. As you can imagine, with four dead young officers, it was a serious affair. We discovered that Davis had stolen a camper. The owner called it in once he woke up from a pistol-whipping, and the SWAT team spotted the camper at about 3:30 in the morning and made the arrest.

I was on the team going after Twining. He had fled to Lyons Avenue, behind a Denny's restaurant, and broken into a home belonging to the Hoag family. The wife and the 17-year-old son escaped, but Twining held the husband hostage. For the next several hours, negotiators talked on the phone with Twining, who bragged about how he had taken advantage of Frago's mistake in carrying his gun at port. "He got careless, so I wasted him."

All night, I was on a hillside overlooking the house, armed with a .308 rifle on sniper duty. Twining held the hostage for six hours.

Aerial view of the Hoag residence

I was on sniper duty on that hillside behind the house for most of the night.

SEB in front of the house

The sun rose, and finally, around 9 a.m., Twining released his hostage from the house. We issued a surrender ultimatum and, when there was no response, pumped tear gas into the structure. My teammates stormed in as I kept an eye on all the entrances, my rifle at the ready. But I never had to use it.

Here, SEB officers prepare to teargas the residence and enter.

I heard the shots fired inside the house. First one and then a stream of them. As the deputies entered the home, Twining turned his gun on himself and committed suicide. That didn't stop every one of the eight deputies from putting more bullets into him to ensure he was dead. It all happened very quickly. When I saw the body in the house, it barely resembled a human anymore.

Demise of killer, Jack Twining

As for his captured accomplice, Bobby Davis was sentenced to die in the gas chamber, but in 1972 the California Supreme Court declared the death penalty to be cruel and unusual punishment and in 1973, the court modified Davis's sentence to life in prison. In 2009 he died in the Kern Valley State Prison of apparent suicide.

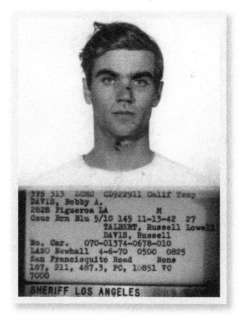

Bobbie Davis
AKA Russell
Talbert, age 27

CHAPTER 12

Crazy Charlie Manson

O F ALL THE CRAZY PEOPLE I've encountered, Charlie Manson may have been the craziest. But it turns out that if you give homeless, runaway teenagers with nothing going for them sex, food, drugs, and a sense of belonging and purpose, however skewed and strange, they will love you. That's how Charles Manson formed The Family.

By the time he became a pseudo-cult leader, Charlie had already spent over half his 32 years in prison and other institutions. He was a serial criminal, having been involved in theft, fraud, grand larceny—mostly for stealing cars—pimping, and more. His annual reviews noted that, among other things, he had a "tremendous drive to call attention to himself."

Charles Manson's mugshot, 1956.

After serving a ten-year sentence, Charlie was released in March 1967. Reportedly, he asked prison officials to let him remain in prison, but with his term completed, they denied his request. He went to San Francisco, where he ended up under the eye of a probation officer and criminal doctoral researcher named Roger Smith, who worked at the Haight-Ashbury Free Medical Clinic. Smith was studying the effects of LSD and methamphetamines on the counterculture movement in the Haight. He conducted regular studies on Manson and a few female followers the ex-felon had already attracted. With the LSD, Charlie reinvented himself as a guru-philosopher-type who targeted teenage runaways and other lost souls, particularly attractive young women he used for sex and bartered to others. He started "preaching" strange philosophies—smashing together bits of the *Bible*, Scientology, Dale Carnegie, free love, the book *Stranger in a Strange Land*, and song lyrics by the Beatles. Psychedelic drugs, especially those that impaired judgment and altered reality gave him more control over the young people he collected than ever before.

After amassing some twenty followers, he moved his cult to Los Angeles. One of his followers was the daughter of actress Angela Lansbury. Having met Manson briefly and sensing danger, Lansbury moved her family to Ireland to get away. Her daughter was one of the lucky ones, though the family struggled for a time after the incident.

One of the reasons Charlie went to L.A. was to become a "rock star." He fancied himself a musician and wanted a record contract. While incarcerated between 1960 and 1967, Charlie had learned how to play the guitar from members of the Barker-Karpis Gang, Depression-era gangsters. Once in Los Angeles and a natural self-promoter, Manson crossed paths with several influential people in the music industry, including members of the Beach Boys, producer Terry Melcher, Neil Young, and Mama Cass. He was crazy, but he was also persistent and known to be charismatic. Later, I had close contact with him and found his charisma to be less than impressive, but I suppose he had a gift for charming people.

Manson broke into the inner circle of the music scene somewhat by chance. Beach Boys band member Dennis Wilson picked up a couple of girls hitchhiking in Malibu—he was in the habit of picking up hitchhikers during that time. The girls were Manson Family members, including Patricia Krenwinkel, who later participated in seven murders. They introduced Dennis, who was doing a lot of drugs at the time, to Charlie. He fell under Charlie's spell for a short time, and the Family took over his cars and the house he was renting. He helped Charlie get an audition with record producer Terry Melcher, whose mother was actress Doris Day. Terry even recorded the Beach Boys playing one of Charlie's songs, originally called "Cease to Exist," and reworked to become "Never Learn Not to Love."

Never Learn not to Love.

When Charlie auditioned, Melcher declined to sign him. He had witnessed Charlie fighting with a drunken stuntman at Spahn Movie Ranch and said, "Don't let the door hit your backside when you leave." The Ranch was where Manson and the Family had settled in, an out-of-the-way place in the Chatsworth area, located inland, in the hills near Malibu. It was a movie set for silent Westerns and 1950s and 1960s television shows like *The Lone Ranger* and *Bonanza*.

Charlie was not happy about getting ditched by Melcher. He wanted to retaliate against the producer and scare him. Melcher and his girlfriend, actress Candice Bergen, were renting a place at

10050 Cielo Drive in Los Angeles when Manson met him. Shortly after, they vacated the house. The owner then leased the house to Roman Polanski and his pregnant wife, actress Sharon Tate. The rest is well-known.

Manson wasn't there, but on his behalf, on August 6, 1969, members of the Family tortured and killed Sharon and her unborn child. They also killed Jay Sebring, a noted celebrity hairstylist; Polanski's friend Wojciech Frykowski and his girlfriend Abigail Folger, heiress to the Folgers coffee fortune; and Steven Parent, who had come to stay in the caretaker's cottage. Polanski was out of the country. The Family wrote "Kill the Pigs" on the wall in Sharon Tate's blood.

The next day, Charlie and members of the Family killed supermarket executive Leno and Rosemary LaBianca in their home. They lived next door to a place where Manson and his followers had partied a number of times. According to one version of events, the young roommates in the house had refused to allow Manson to move in during the fall of 1968, and this so infuriated Manson that he sought revenge. Either they weren't home the night of the murders, or Charlie chose their next-door neighbors as a scare tactic.

The Family wrote "Rise" and "Death to Pigs" on the wall and "Helter Skelter" (misspelled) on the refrigerator door. Charlie had become a white supremacist, and the words were an attempt to frame the murders on Black people. He told his followers that Black people in America were going to rise up and kill all white people except for Manson and The Family. Sick stuff.

The murders were an LAPD case. They had no idea who the suspects were. None of the victims appeared to have any enemies.

In an unrelated incident at the time, our Special Enforcement Bureau was contacted by the Malibu Sheriff's Station. They said an automobile theft ring was working out of the old Spahn Movie Ranch, and they required assistance. In developing the operation to surround the Ranch, we learned that the ring comprised both hippie types and members of the Satan's Slaves motorcycle gang, all of whom had invaded the ranch with the tacit approval of the aging owner, George Spahn. His grandson, alarmed at the state of things when he visited his grandfather at the ranch, reported the ring to the Sheriff's Department. "They're victimizing my grandfather," he said. "He's in his eighties!"

George Spahn at the ranch, age 81. Photo by Jim Harris.

We were fortunate to have an informant working with us, a person who had been staying there and left the ranch worked with us. He told us that numerous runaway juveniles were staying at the ranch and identified on an aerial photo the building where the runaways were staying. He also alerted us that some individuals at the ranch were carrying firearms and had people stationed at lookout posts that might sound the alarm if they saw police vehicles arrive. And he identified one of the leaders by name, an ex-con by the name of Charles Manson, who was also armed.

The Malibu Sheriff's Department acquired a search warrant for the property and for a personal search of Manson. That's all we knew at the time. Our operation relied on support from the Emergency Services Detail, Narcotics, Intelligence, Aero, and Special Units bureaus, the Sheriff's Information Bureau, and the Los Angeles County Fire Department, a coordinated operation.

We went in on August 17. My duty as part of the SWAT team was to maintain outside security. I had my sniper rifle with me. Officers arrested twenty-six people, including Manson, who was hiding in a crawlspace under one of the ranch buildings. Our SEB leader, John Kolman, described Manson in his report as "filthy, unkempt, slovenly, and smelly," as was the rest of The Family.

Looking for Charlie

The squalor they were living in was unbelievable. Our forces found many stolen vehicles and confiscated numerous firearms, including a World War II-era German sub-machine gun housed in a violin case.

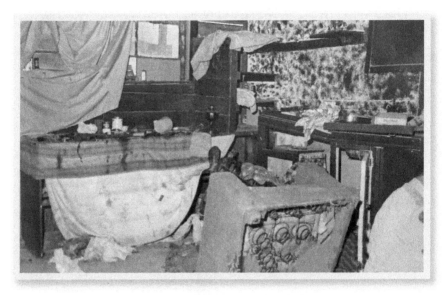

Living conditions on Spahn Ranch

The World War II-era German sub-machine gun housed in a violin case, one of many confiscated firearms.

Under arrest at the ranch: Manson, "Straight Satan" gang member Robert Reinhard and ranch hand Juan Flynn

Deputies with three of the younger family members

At that time, we still didn't tie the killings to Manson. We arrested him for grand theft auto, illegal firearms, and drug possession. I was surprised when the case was kicked out of court. There are two accounts as to why. One is that the DA had screwed up on the search warrant. It was misdated. The other was that a deputy district attorney refused to charge any of the arrestees because it could not be proven who was responsible for stealing the recovered vehicles.

So, all the Manson suspects beat feet to the remote Barker Ranch, out by Death Valley. Manson promised his followers that Barker Ranch would provide them a safe haven from a coming apocalypse where they would emerge as leaders of the new America. Mrs. Barker rented her ranch to the Manson Family, thinking they were a group of musicians who needed space to practice.

While there, Manson's followers conducted raids in Death Valley, stealing dune buggies and vandalizing National Park property. These relatively petty crimes led to the Manson Family's second arrest. When a joint force of the Inyo County Sheriff's Department, California Highway Patrol, and the National Park Service raided the ranch on October 10 and October 12, 1969, and dragged a crazed, Swastika-tattooed man out from under a bathroom vanity, they thought they were nabbing a group of local troublemakers. It soon became clear that the Manson Family was much more than that.

In November, following extensive investigations and numerous interviews of in-custody and released Manson Family members, the connection to the Tate/LaBianca and several other murders was established. The first trial of members of the Manson Family— Patricia Krenwinkel, Susan Atkins, and Leslie Van Houten—began in July 1970. They were held in the county jail system, and we had security. My job, along with several other officers, was to escort Charles Manson to court.

Charlie was a short little dude, just five-foot-two. He was also a talker. Manson, David Koresh, Jim Jones, and Hitler were all good talkers. We kept a tape recorder going as we walked Charlie to the courthouse in handcuffs.

I said, "Charlie, did you kill Gary Hinman?" He was an earlier homicide victim.

He said, "No, I just cut his ear off."

Charlie was acting stupid all day long in court. He made faces, fidgeted, and had repeated outbursts that got him kicked out of the room temporarily. He once said to the judge, "You've got your flunkies. It would be a different story if it was just you and I."

The Family members who had not been arrested kept chanting in the background until they were dismissed from

Charlie in court
Photo by Moses Armstrong

the room. At one point, Manson announced that he wished to testify. He said, "The children that come at you with knives are your children. You taught them. I didn't teach them. I only tried to help them stand up...." He was just insane.

Some members of The Family that weren't arrested sat outside the Hall of Justice jail in a brown Ford van. Since they stayed out there all night, we were assigned to watch them. We didn't think they could break the others out of jail, but we didn't want to take any chances. After two or three hours of surveillance, at about three in the morning, one of my fellow deputies had had enough. He got a cherry bomb and threw it at the van. The explosion must've scared the pants off of them. The van took off, and we went home.

167

During the trial, one of Charlie's girls, seventeen-year-old Dianne Lake, who had left the Family, came forward to testify. After escaping Spahn Ranch, she had been in a state hospital for drug psychosis from overuse. Another key witness was Linda Kasabian. She had been present at the murders and testified in exchange for an immunity offer.

The most important witness was Leslie Van Houten, one of the girls on trial for murder. She had this attorney named Ronald Hughes, who had failed the bar exam three times before passing and had never tried a case. Some called him "the hippie lawyer." He was short, with a big beer belly and an untrimmed beard—not at all like most lawyers. He lived in a dirty garage that belonged to a friend, sleeping on a mattress on the floor. Originally, Hughes wanted to represent Manson but was replaced at the last minute.

Manson girls on trial, Patricia Krenwinkel, Leslie Van Houten, and Susan Atkins. Photo by John Malmin

Hughes' inexperience showed when the trial first began, but by the trial's midpoint, Prosecutor Vince Bugliosi, who wrote the best-selling book about Manson called *Helter Skelter*, said he thought he was doing "damn well." Hughes' intimate knowledge of the hippie subculture sometimes served his client well. For example, he raised questions about Linda Kasabian's credibility by asking her about hallucinogenic drugs, her belief in ESP, her thoughts that she might be a witch, and her experiencing "vibrations" from Charles Manson. Hughes tried to separate the interests of his client, defendant Leslie Van Houten, from those of Manson and show that she was not acting independently but was completely controlled in her actions by Charlie. He suggested she testify against him and the Family as part of a plea bargain.

Then, in the midst of the trial during the last weekend of November 1970, Hughes disappeared while camping in a remote area near Sespe Hot Springs. His badly decomposed body was not discovered until four months later. Although no one was ever charged with the murder of Hughes, at least two Family members admitted later that the killing of Hughes was a "retaliation murder" by Manson Family members, including Squeaky Fromme, who later tried to assassinate President Gerald Ford. Van Houten got a new attorney and changed her mind. She didn't want to testify

Staff Photo by Bob Carrington

That's me with Manson Family members released on bail.

anymore against Manson and The Family. The trial continued, and Manson, the three girls, and later, Tex Watson in a separate trial, received the death penalty.

In October, A lifelong criminal named Ken Como met members of the Manson Family in the Hall of Justice while they were there awaiting trial, and he joined The Family while in custody. Como had been transferred from Folsom Prison to testify in a murder trial. He was a member of the Aryan Brotherhood. What a lot of people may not know is that Manson had direct ties with the AB. The AB agreed to provide protection to Manson in prison, shielding him from the Black gangs. In exchange, Manson encouraged the female members of The Family to act as "comfort aides" to incarcerated Aryan Brotherhood members by sending the men sexy photos of themselves.

Having escaped several Los Angeles County jails, Como escaped again when he was in the holding cell at the Hall of Records before his trial. He and another convict tied jail clothes together to form a rope and lowered themselves out a window. Como met up with six other Family members and masterminded a robbery of the Western Surplus Store in Hawthorne to gather a full arsenal of weapons to free Manson. An employee was able to trip a silent alarm, and after a shoot-out and a manhunt for Como, the Hawthorne police arrested all seven suspects.

Using hacksaws smuggled into him and tying together his clothes to make a rope, Como escaped one more time from the 13th floor of the Hall of Justice. He was picked up by Family Member Sandy Good, who crashed her car and was arrested. Como spent a few hours on the lam in a neighborhood between Hollywood and Sunset. Members of our SEB team were brought in. Finally, after seven hours, my colleagues Donnie Dunlap and Roger Anderson—the first a retired stuntman and bodybuilder, the latter a black belt in karate—found Como in a storage cabinet. You can bet they weren't going to let him escape again!

Como was arraigned in Inglewood Court by Judge Lynch.

Judge Lynch knew what was going on. He knew that the existing Family members or the Aryan Brotherhood were a real threat to his safety and to the safety of everyone in that courtroom. The judge had a gun but had no bullets. I was working in the courtroom that day, and he asked me for bullets for protection. I gave him six. What was I going to tell a judge? Go pound sand? He kept the gun under his robe in court throughout the trial. Fortunately, there was no retaliation during the indictment, and Como went to prison and died there in 2004.

Ken Como, escorted for the last time, by SEB Deputies Jim Cox, Don Dunlop, and Roger Anderson.

CHAPTER 13

The Isla Vista Riot

I
N 1970, THE CONFLICT IN VIETNAM RAGED, and young
American men were being drafted to fight. The United States'
involvement in the war became increasingly unpopular,
especially among young people. There was an air of distrust of the
establishment. Side by side with Flower Power preaching peace
and love, anarchists declared that state authority and individual
autonomy were mutually exclusive. Protests were commonplace on
college campuses and spilled into the streets, occasionally becoming
riots, even in the sleepy oceanfront college town of Isla Vista, home
of students attending UC Santa Barbara.

It's strange watching the rise of a riot. Crowds of people form
for whatever reason—an event or a disturbance—and an existing
underlying tension rises to the surface, triggered by some sort of
action or incident—large, small, or even unrelated, but usually
violent. And that unleashes the emotion. A wave of anger and fear
and confusion moves through the crowd. Then comes panic, and
with it fight or flight, looting, and increased violence.

Our SWAT team was called into Isla Vista four times in 1970
when the Sheriff's Department in Santa Barbara was quickly
overwhelmed by protests that turned into riots. We arrived along

with 60 L.A. County deputies. I knew Santa Barbara and Isla Vista well since I used to work there and knew many of the local deputies. These were generally good guys, but they didn't have the training we did.

Keeping the peace on the UC Santa Barbara campus, February 1970

Riot #1: January 30 to February 3

The first time was in January when an ousted Anthropology professor, a leader of dissident groups on campus, closed down the UCSB Administration Building. The Regents and local Law Enforcement were expecting hundreds if not thousands of students to protest the next day. They didn't have training for that or the manpower, so they called us in.

When we arrived, Santa Barbara sheriffs' deputies were having Wham-o slingshot fights with the demonstrators, slinging marbles at each other. It was crazy! Since chemical agents were forbidden, the Santa Barbara County Sheriff deemed the slingshots "reasonable and necessary force."

The potentially deadly "wrist rocket" slingshot with ball bearings or marbles used in Isla Vista. And a toy pistol that almost resulted in the shooting of its owner.

Luckily, all we had to do was be an organized presence in uniform on campus. The weather turned cold, and the crowd dispersed independently.

Riot #2: February 25 to 28

Early in the afternoon on February 25, 1970, defense attorney William Kunstler spoke at the UC Santa Barbara campus stadium. He represented the defendants in the Chicago Seven trial following the anti-war protests at the 1968 Democratic National Convention.

It was a provocative presentation, and, anticipating another inflammatory reaction, we were called in again to control the crowd.

The protest by hundreds of people was peaceful for at least an hour following Kunstler's speech, although as in January, there was a lot of incendiary talk, lots of yelling at us. On the SEB team, we were trained not to respond to stuff like that.

But as one group of students marched back toward Isla Vista after the speech, local police accosted, beat, and arrested 22-year-old Rich Underwood. They thought he was carrying a Molotov cocktail. It turned out to be a bottle of wine. Word got around. When one of our patrol car traveled around the loop, a couple of guys started yelling and threw a rock at the car. Within minutes, they were joined by others throwing whatever was around. Upon reaching the Francisco Torres towers, known now as Santa Catalina dorms, many students donned handkerchiefs and rocks armed to hurl at us.

By late afternoon, the riot had spread into the community of Isla Vista, adjacent to the campus with probably 1,000 people on the streets. A few of the unruly mob threw rocks at the windows and doors of some of the businesses. One particularly anarchist group

had taken possession of a police car, turned it over on its hood and set it on fire. Another group of protesters made their base next to the Bank of America, displaying a handmade sign that read "Pig Patrol." The Isla Vista branch of the Bank of America became the main target of the rioting because it was funding Apartheid in South Africa and had ties to the defense industry. It was the only bank in town known to be stingy on student loans. To the activists, all of these reasons and more made the bank a symbol of the capitalist establishment that benefited from the war and oppressed people worldwide in the interests of the government. There was a popular

poster at the time, referencing the USSR, that said, "Don't Bank on Amerika." I even had one in my Manhattan Beach apartment. During the afternoon, attempts were made to enter the bank, including breaking down the plywood panel that covered the doors. A small fire was set inside the door, causing minor charring of the framing.

Later in the evening, some antiwar activists and anarchists took radical action. They pushed a large dumpster on wheels into the street in front of the bank and lit its contents on fire. The dumpster was then pushed through the bank's front door, where it came to rest immediately inside the doorway. Once inside the bank, it flamed intensely for a short while, causing charring and smoke damage to the structure. The fire in the dumpster was extinguished and removed. Shortly thereafter, a large crowd entered the bank through a rear door and proceeded to destroy records, tip over furniture, and set more small fires. Around midnight, the dumpster was again pushed inside the bank, and gas was used to rekindle the fire. The bank was destroyed.

Protesters in Perfect Park, Isla Vista, when it was still peaceful

The more radical protesters gathered in Perfect Park (based on People's Park near UC Berkeley), and Santa Barbara Sheriff's Department officers shot teargas over their heads to get the students out, but the wind blew the teargas back toward the deputies. Fellow officers had to do a low crawl with extra gas masks to pull the officers out of a white pickup truck where they had taken cover.

As SEB, we took care of business. We lined up in our riot gear and then moved together as one. No one said anything; we just went. We cleared that park of 500 people in thirty seconds, only arresting those who threatened violence.

Then we went patrolling, working in three-man cars. We learned that from the Watts riots. One man acted as the car guard while the other two deputies handled the situation. It was important to protect the car from damage and prevent theft of equipment or weaponry. In the middle of a riot, people lose all judgment. Tony Welch was our car guard, while Dicky Madden and I went into action. The first guy we arrested threw a rock about the size of a softball at us from a second-story window. It could have killed one of us if it had hit us in the head. We kicked in the door when he refused to let us into his apartment. He was hiding behind the shower curtain and refused to come out. When I grabbed him, he tried to kick me. I hooked

177

him up and dragged him down the stairs. He turned out to be an exchange student from Germany. He was deported for his actions. That was my first of many arrests that night. Overall, we arrested 300 to 400 people before we were relieved by the National Guard.

But that wasn't the end of it. We were called back to Isla Vista in April and in June.

I am on the left, in action with a fellow SEB officer.

Isla Vista Riot #3: April 16 to 21

In April, students were throwing Molotov cocktails and starting more fires, especially at businesses. Tired of the anarchy, other students tried to put out the fires. A 22-year-old UCSB economics major named Kevin Moran and his roommates had squelched a fire at a Taco Bell before they put out yet another fire at what was left of the Bank of America. Moran was accidentally shot and killed by Santa Barbara officer David Gosselin. The officer was wearing gloves because of the cold and misfired. Although he was never indicted, Gosselin took full responsibility and, traumatized by the event, left the force of his own free will.

A mandatory curfew was ordered for the town. One deputy told me he saw one female student in her yard barbecuing a steak. He told her, "Get in your house," and then ate her steak. Not the finest behavior, but it seemed funny at the time. Later, when I retired and moved, I met the woman by coincidence. She said, "I was that lady. I was pregnant with my daughter." She frowned. "Those guys ate my steak!" Her son, Ryan, and my son ended up on the same ski team and went to high school together. There are many perspectives of any incidence.

Isla Vista Riot #4: June 4 to 12

Each time we were called in to stop disturbances in Isla Vista, we spent the day and night patrolling, and the disturbance was over by morning. It was terrible that the one young man was killed. But as far as I know, only a few other people got seriously hurt.

Then the FBI got involved and made matters worse. On June 3, 1970, the Grand Jury of Santa Barbara County indicted fifteen people on felony and misdemeanor charges. It turned out that two of them had absolute alibis. Several were juveniles. Four were ultimately found guilty of misdemeanors. It was national news. The timing of the indictments was terrible. They should've waited until summer.

It led to a week-long riot of window-smashing and arson by anarchists who roamed through the area around the Bank of America's temporary structure. Moderate-minded students continued fighting with the extremists. It was a mess when we were called in on the third day of that final riot. Perpetrators had placed caltrops, heavy-gauge wire with points, on the streets to flatten our tires. They continued to throw things at our cars.

A confiscated caltrop. Protesters also used boards spiked with nails.

179

Changing a tire flattened by a caltrops

*One crew's arrests on the first day
of the June riots.*

Then Governor Ronald Reagan took action. He ordered the National Guard into Isla Vista and instituted a curfew. According to one investigator with the *New York Times*, the state had called in a dozen different units under different commands and with different attitudes. I don't know about other law enforcement agencies, but as far as I was concerned, our job in the SEB was to make arrests, not to brutalize, beat, or harm people. We were resolute in our duties. It was a riot, and we treated it as such. If a student was out past curfew, we took her in. When someone didn't cooperate, we used force to cuff him. But not everyone there was trained like us.

Many of the population in Isla Vista were young, privileged, white college kids. Their parents had political sway. Faculty and local clergymen organized teams of observers to note and keep meticulous records of the conduct of the anarchists and the police. They claimed 213 complaints against law enforcement from the June riot. Sixty-seven of the complaints were against our Special Enforcement Bureau. Dr. James J. Sullivan, an economics teacher who headed the program, acknowledged that many of these reflected exaggeration or cynical contrivances. The young tend to be dramatic. The media loves controversy. There was also the evidence of fires burning, tires flattened, rocks thrown, and other acts of violence and resistance by protesters.

But in the end, that didn't matter. Sheriff Pitchess transferred all of us, every man, except two—eighty well-trained officers to satisfy public outcry and political pressure. We were scapegoated out.

For the time being, the SWAT team was gone, to be reformed a year later with all new personnel. Pitchess' political move affected all of us.

I was transferred back to the transportation

Debriefing with the SEB team on June 12, and perhaps enjoying an adult beverage, at the Holiday Inn in Isla Vista after a long week. We didn't know it would be the end of our tenure on the SWAT team.

Me, leaving our headquarters at the Holiday Inn

unit. I still kept my rank, but the work was menial compared to the previous two and a half years. It was severely disappointing, to say the least. As a team, we were especially disappointed in Sheriff

Isla Vista: A Changing Tide Engulfs Officers

93 Elite L.A. Sheriff's Men Who Halted Riot Are Reassigned, Many to Menial Positions

BY DIAL TORGERSON
Times Staff Writer

The tides of fortune have turned again in Isla Vista.

Snatched from the law by a rock-throwing, window-smashing, bank-burning mob, Isla Vista was reclaimed for law and order by the batons of Los Angeles County's toughest sheriff's officers.

The 93 men of the sheriff's Special Enforcement Bureau arrested most of the almost 700 young men and women jailed in the bloody week of disturbances in June of 1970.

But, despite their success—and, in a way, because of it—the 93 men who ended the last of three wild Isla Vista rio's have been reassigned

Angeles federal attorney was then in charge of the grand jury inquiry into charges of overreaction by the SEB.

But the decision to turn transcripts over to the authorities in Santa Barbara for possible legal action —as will be done this week—was not reached until June 15. Mitchell and Pitchess met in Washington June 3.

The sheriff's office emphatically denies that any kind of a deal was made between Pitchess and Mitchell whereby there would be no federal prosecution if Pitchess disciplined his own men. A Justice Department spokesman said in Washingto[...]

This was a very different population than in Watts, and as a result, it got political.

Pitchess' response to the media when asked why the transfers took place.

"We were not entirely satisfied with the overall performance of the SEB, and haven't been for some time," he said in the *Los Angeles Times*. But if that was true, wouldn't we have heard about it sooner?

His criticism was in direct contrast to a

Isla Vista: Tide Engulfs Sheriff's Men

Continued from 28th Page

official, whose son was in Isla Vista in June of 1970.

"It's like the case of a soldier overseas. The farther he gets away from home the more his respect for people and property diminishes. Then, too, these officers were being set upon from the tops of buildings with rocks, bottles of urine and taunts.

"It was a highly emotional situation. There's a breaking point. Officers are human. There is supposed to be one supervisor for each seven men in a tactical outfit like this, and many times this was

182

28 Los Angeles Times 2★
Part I—Thurs., June 11, 1970

Complaints of Brutality by Police Mount

Continued from First Page

Until Wednesday night, 300 persons had been jailed in Isla Vista since militants began disturbances here last Thursday night, when 17 persons were indicted by a grand jury on charges stemming from earlier Isla Vista violence.

The community of 13,000 has been subjected to numerous curfews since a gang burned a Bank of America branch in February. The curfew, imposed from 7:30 p.m. to 6 a.m., and enforced by heavily armed law officers, resulted in most of the latest series of arrests.

One businessman in Isla Vista claimed that last week there were only 50 militants in Isla Vista who wanted to see the bank branch burned as a "symbol of the establishment." He said early Wednesday: "Now there are 500."

The enforcement of the curfew provoked its own violence. As sheriff's and California Highway Patrol cars rolled in four-car patrols, lights out, through Isla Vista streets, youths set off flaming garbage containers in their path, then hurled rocks at the cars.

But members of the community who surveyed the lists of names of those arrested — a record 142 Tuesday night and Wednesday morning — said that few of those jailed were the street-wise militants who stoned and burned.

Among the persons arrested, booked, and jailed were:

Doug McMeen ("the most studious fellow on the block") was trying to walk home from the campus computer center Tuesday night, carrying his briefcase full of papers he was preparing for his final exams, when officers arrested him on a charge of

Isla Vista Free Methodist Church Wednesday, speakers were especially critical of the Los Angeles County Sheriff's Department's special enforcement bureau, which loaned 80 officers to Santa Barbara.

Rob Perelli, a UCSB student who has been active in attempting to thwart militant attempts against the bank branch for the past two months, said he was struck with a baton and that he and his girlfriend were dragged down the stairs of his apartment by the hair by a Los Angeles deputy he identified as "McPherson, Badge 3137."

Brutality Charge

Another youth, Gary Earle, said Los Angeles officers broke into his apartment, bound his hands behind him, and placed him in a squad car, where one officer hit him in the jaw, splitting open the skin. After he was booked and put in a bus, a deputy kicked him in the groin, he said. He identified the officers as O'Mullin, Mead and Harrison.

The information bureau of the Los Angeles sher-

ARRESTS — Scene in front of the battered Isla Vista bank as young people their hands tied, are booked by sheriff's deputies on violations of the curfew
Times photo by Fitzgerald Whitney

My name made the front page of the L.A. Times, although I didn't do what they said I did. That was another deputy.

183

comment in the press made by the legal affairs secretary for then-Governor Reagan on June 11: "We probably couldn't have done the job without them (SEB)."

Thirty members of our staff were reassigned first, on June 21. Sergeant Kolman in our unit sent a well-intended letter to Sheriff Pitchess to protest their removal. I don't know if it did nothing or made matters worse, but the Sergeant always felt responsible for the remaining 35 officers that were "routinely" transferred one week later.

But that's the way it goes sometimes. Still, I celebrate those two and half years working SEB with the SWAT team.

This parody letter pretty much sums up how we felt.

Please refer
To file No. 86

June 7, 1971

TO: All Personnel

SUBJECT: Program to Facilitate the Termination of Present
         S.E.B. (Special Enforcement Bureau) Personnel

In a moment of rage it was decided that present personnel should be transferred and labeled 'S.O.B.s" (Surplus Old Personnel).

In accordance with Department policy, a new program has been instituted to phase out present S.E.B. personnel by the end of June, namely, RAPE (Replace All Personnel Early), effective immediately.

Deputies who are RAPE'D will not be given the opportunity to transfer to the assignment of their choice, but may request a review of their transfer after they are RAPE'D. The review is called SCREW (Survey of Capabilities of Replaced Early Worker).

All employees who have been RAPE'D and SCREW'D may appeal for a final review. This will be called SHAFT (Study of Higher Authority Following Transfer).

Present policy dictates that S.E.B., S.O.B.s may be RAPE'D once and SCREW'D twice, but may get the SHAFT as many times as the Department deems appropriate.

CHAPTER 14

Two Years in Malibu, 1971–1972

W E WERE FORCED TO DO PENANCE FOR our alleged misdeeds in Isla Vista. We could not transfer back once our group was transferred off of SWAT. We could only transfer back to regular deputy patrol. It was really disappointing. The closest place to my home in Camarillo was the Malibu station. The Undersheriff, Bob Edmunds, the second-highest guy in law enforcement in L.A. County, was a good friend of mine. At my request, he sent me to Malibu.

Malibu is a beach town that runs along the Pacific Ocean and extends up into the hills. It's home to surfers, celebrities, lucky locals, and vacation homes. It is a beautiful area. In the 1970s, it was an untamed place of free love, drugs, and a growing community of wealthy homeowners. Malibu was incorporated into a city on March 28, 1991.

Celebrities on the Beat

We had our share of celebrity sightings in Malibu. It was an exclusive place with some of the best beaches in California, so it was no wonder it attracted the rich and famous. Some of the houses were so big they extended over the cliffs with stairs down to their own private stretch of beach. You had to know where to go to find the hidden semi-private beaches. Even now, there are entrances where you need a special key to get past the gate and down to the beach. They don't want any regular people in their exclusive playground.

While working in Malibu, meeting Hollywood actors, powerful CEOs, or other prominent and influential people was a fairly common occurrence, both on and off the job. Bad stuff can happen to celebrities, too. After all, they're people, just like the rest of us.

In a bar one night, one of my friends introduced me to Carroll Shelby, the race car driver, designer and builder. They made a movie about him called *Ford vs. Ferrari*, and Matt Damon played him. Back then, he was just an unassuming guy who wore a cowboy hat and was very welcoming. I only talked to him for five minutes, but being a car guy, I was thrilled. I had gotten rid of a '65 GTO Pontiac that took forever to stop because the brakes were terrible. We used to joke that GTO stood for gas, tires, and oil.

One of the deputies I worked with was the son of Actress Betty Hutton, who played the lead in *Annie Get Your Gun*, a bunch of other movies, and her own TV show. When she died, he quit the department because he inherited a bunch of money and didn't have to work anymore.

Another of our reserve deputies I often served with was Van Williams, an actor who played the Green Hornet on television in 1966–67, along with his sidekick Kato, played by a young Bruce Lee. He was also in a couple detective series. In his free time, Williams also worked for the search and rescue team. He told me some great stories while riding along on my beat. He said that

Bruce Lee could move so rapidly they had to slow down the film, including when filming his famous one-finger push-ups. Van also had dated several starlets, not to be named.

We had another reserve we called a "lucky sperm recipient." He had inherited wealth and never had to work a day in his life. His father or grandfather invented those spun aluminum lines on plumbing features used in washing

Van Williams as the Green Hornet and Bruce Lee as Kato.

machines, toilets, car lines, race cars because they don't break. But I admired that despite his social position, he was never showy with his wealth and worked hard as a volunteer with the department. He did splurge on a 1948 Porsche Spider, the same kind that James Dean died in. It was a gorgeous car that he displayed at the annual car show in Malibu.

The actor Robert Stack lived in Malibu. He was very pro-police and frequently talked to detectives and deputies. Once, he even came into the station when he had some information on a rape suspect. He saw the suspect drive away from the crime scene and identified the guy's green Pontiac. The information led to the suspect's arrest. Actor Mark Harmon, best known for his role as Leroy Jethro Gibbs in *NCIS*, also lived in Malibu. I met him once. He was taller than me, had very blue eyes, and was impressive and handsome. His father, Tom Harmon, was a famous football player at the University of Michigan. His mother was Elyse Knox, the movie actress. Like his father, Mark played football in college for the UCLA Bruins—and you could tell.

Hervé Villechaize

Hervé Villechaize came into the station a couple of times on business. He was born with dwarfism and stood just three feet eleven inches tall. He's probably best remembered as Tattoo, the sidekick to Ricardo Montalbán on *Fantasy Island* (1977–1984), and as the evil henchman Nick Nack in the 1974 James Bond film, *The Man with the Golden Gun*. But at that time, his only credits were *The Gang that Couldn't Shoot Straight* and some other B-movies and off-Broadway shows.

I remember his fingertips could hardly reach the railing on the stairs or the top of the station desktop. I don't remember why he was there. Maybe it was because Villechaize was an active member of a movement in the 1970s and 1980s in California to deal with child abuse and neglect. He listened to police reports on the radio. He went to crime scenes where child abuse was reported to help comfort the victims. After speaking to officers at the station, he left abruptly, saying he had some business to take care of. I watched him leave. Outside the station, he climbed into a waiting Cadillac with two very attractive ladies and sat between them in a child's safety seat. It was a strange sight but impressive nonetheless. He was reputed to be a serious ladies' man.

Residents of Malibu tended to drive very nice cars. I was always looking for Porsches when I patrolled because people would steal and strip them. Outside a private residence near the Malibu Cold Colony restaurant, an upscale place on the ocean, I saw a purple Porsche Targa. The license plate read CHER. You can guess who that belonged to.

Our station was on the Pacific Coast Highway, near Malibu Canyon, just below Pepperdine University. Some very upscale homes were located between the station and the college. Some years later as a detective I was back patrolling that neighborhood when I saw a Porsche 911 silver coupe with another unusual plate number: X8618X. It was parked in front of a large home. I got out of the squad car to take a better look. The front door opened, and the guy who bounded down the stairs was Bruce Jenner. He explained that 8618 was his Olympic point total. It was shortly after he had won the gold medal in the decathlon at the 1976 Olympics in Moscow, becoming known as the "World's Greatest Athlete." He'd become an American hero, appearing on magazine covers, TV shows, and the Wheaties cereal box. In 2015, he would come out as a transgender woman and change her name to Caitlyn, but I knew him as Bruce at the time. We talked about cars for a while. He loved cars like I did and went on to race them for a while. He was taller than me and a soft-spoken, nice guy with a good attitude toward the police. It was a memorable moment.

Halloween Hijinks & Parenting Styles

One of my first Malibu calls on the new beat in 1971 was on Halloween night. Two fifteen-year-old boys were throwing eggs at cars. The sulfur in raw eggs takes the paint right off of cars. When my partner and I caught up to these little darlings, we found them showing a John Holmes-size dildo to some ten-year-old girls. The boys were being disrespectful in multiple ways. My partner and I confiscated their eggs and the 10-inch dildo and asked the boys some questions. It was clear that these kids didn't need to go to juvie and would get nothing out of that experience, but they did need to learn boundaries. We wanted them to learn a valuable lesson and not harm little girls like that again. So, spontaneously, my partner and I broke the eggs over their heads. Of course, we could never do that today. Even then, I knew we would get jammed for our actions, meaning we would likely get a complaint from dear old mom and dad. These kids were wealthy and privileged, but we had our evidence.

Our station captain, Gary Osborne, was with us when the parents arrived the next day. They were hotter than a firecracker. "How could you do this to our boys?" They asked. I said, "Excuse me, Captain." I went to my locker, retrieved the dildo, put it on the table, and calmly explained what the kids were doing. I never heard anything else about it. Who knows? Maybe at the end of the day, the parents were happy their kids didn't get arrested, and someone else took care of the consequences. Or maybe the dildo belonged to one of the mothers, who was embarrassed.

Dealing with the offspring of the wealthy and privileged was an education for me. In contrast to those boys, we encountered another kid who was probably headed to jail or juvie in the future. At 2:00 in the morning, fellow deputies brought him in. They had found the thirteen-year-old, long-haired surfer passed out in the middle of the Pacific Coast Highway. The deputies probably saved the kid's life. He could have been run over.

A few hours later, the father came in. He drove a BMW and was wearing a nice suit. I watched as the kid, who had come to, spotted his father, sauntered over to him, and said, "Give me a cigarette." The kid didn't say he was sorry or scared. He didn't say anything else. And what did the father do? He silently gave his son a cigarette. He even lit it for him.

I had two children of my own. I couldn't stay out of it. I said, "Sir, can I talk to you?" I pulled him aside and said, "Your son is a piece of human debris. He's got no respect for you. If he were my son, his ass would be around his neck. All you're doing is throwing money at him. If he's like this at thirteen, wait until he's twenty-one. You should take care of him. It appears you take better care of your car than your son." I left it at that. Who knows if that unsolicited advice made any difference. Maybe not, but the neglect just made me mad.

Characters in Malibu

Even in such a sleepy beach town as Malibu, where the sun shines every day and no one seems to have many cares, there were some strange and memorable characters. People can do weird and stupid things. I was answering the phone at the station one day when a lady called in. It was a cold day, and there was a light dusting of snow on the mountains to the east.

She asked, "Deputy, what's that white stuff on the mountains?"

I couldn't believe it. Sarcastically, I answered, "Madam, there was a plane crash. The plane was full of cocaine." I laughed and hung up the phone. Even if she had never seen snow, why call the sheriff's office?

One afternoon, I was in the station lobby when a man came in and removed all his clothes until he stood before us naked. We hooked him up for indecent exposure. Who knows why he did it?

We had a guy in the jail frequently who was in there for being drunk in public. He was twenty-two years old but looked fifty. His skin was yellow. His liver was gone, riddled with cirrhosis. After he had done his time one night, we let him loose at 7:00 the next morning. He signed to collect all the property he had been arrested with, his wallet, and his saddlebag. I could feel a sewn-in compartment in the bag, so before handing it over, we cut it open to look inside and found a syringe.

I asked him, "You do drugs? Shoot up?" He said no. "Are you a diabetic?" He said no. "Then what do you do with the syringe?"

"I inject 151 rum," he said.

No wonder he looked so bad. He looked like road kill. We had to let him go, but I suspected he wouldn't be around long. He was living a death sentence.

A Military Alternative

We couldn't do much about alcohol abuse since the substance was legal. But drugs were a different matter. Addictive drugs were all over Southern California at the time. Early in Malibu, I worked with another deputy named Kent Napper, who had been at that station for a while. He told me about a young man who was dealing drugs up in Calabasas, and they just couldn't get him. "He's always at it," he said, "Selling marijuana and pills to high school kids. I know he's doing it. I have the info. I know what kind of car he drives, but I just can't catch him."

"Okay," I told him, "No problem. We'll get him."

Calabasas is inland in the West Hills on the other side of the Santa Monica Mountains about 25 minutes from Malibu, located near Westlake Village and Thousand Oaks off Highway 101. Back then, with a smaller population and none of it incorporated into cities, the area was part of our Malibu patrol. It was a high-end, gated community where many Hollywood people lived, like Valerie Harper, who played Rhoda Morgenstern in the *Mary Tyler Moore Show* and had a spin-off show of her own. In the 2020s, residents of Westlake Village included Will Smith, Joe Montana, and Hulk Hogan.

From my SWAT training I knew how to stake out the area, and so I got on it. Finally, one day, we saw the dealer drive by in his car. We tailed him, pulled him over, and as soon as we stopped the engine, we hurried to his car. Sure enough, he had drugs on the seat next to him and was trying to hide them. Since we saw them, we had probable cause to search the car without a warrant and found amphetamines and other pills and marijuana. From the moment he was in cuffs, the suspect cooperated. He was just a "normal-looking" kid with a slight build, not at all obnoxious or resistant as we took him in on possession.

He was found guilty in court. He knew he was in the wrong, supplementing his income by selling drugs to minors. Since he was around 23 years old, it was a first offense, and he was selling only "soft drugs," not heroin or cocaine; the judge gave him a choice: go to jail or go into the military. Suspects often got that choice back then. He chose the military. I'd like to think that it led to much better choices in the kid's future. Judges unfortunately no longer have the authority to make such an offer. The modern U.S. armed forces will not accept just anyone. You have to pass a physical, you have to score high enough on the ASVAB, have a high school diploma, and you have to pass a background check and be eligible for a security clearance. A conviction is almost always a disqualifying factor for enlistment. If convictions or pending charges come up in a background check, recruiters may have some leeway for a waiver if it is a very minor crime. However, if it is a crime for which jail is an allowable punishment, it will make the person ineligible for enlistment. Felons have been prohibited from enlisting in the military since 1968.

We definitely had our fun moments in Malibu. Another deputy, named John O'Brien, and I always played tricks on each other. Once, John put mace on my phone, and my eyes started to water when I picked it up. Another time, he smeared shoe polish on the earpiece, so when I held it up to my ear, it turned black. Of course, I couldn't let him get away with that, so I decided to get him back.

John had a Ford Mustang that he loved, and I knew I could get him good with it. I found these sticky labels that said "Hold for Prints" and "Crime Scene." I covered his entire windshield with the labels. He couldn't see out of the Mustang at all. He had to scrape it all off to be able to drive. John was not too happy with me when he saw his Mustang, but we both laughed about it later. We always enjoyed playing pranks on each other, making the long hours on the job more bearable.

The Thief in a Speedo

The funniest story while I was in Malibu involved a con man and a swimsuit. The story was that he had conned several thousand dollars from a member of the *M*A*S*H* cast. The TV show *M*A*S*H* was being filmed in Malibu at the time. This con man was a white dude who spoke Spanish fluently, was handsome and tan, and supposedly great at tennis. Everyone around Malibu knew him, and he was rumored to be a small-time gangster. We'll call him F.S. One time, F.S. strolled into the Barclays Bank, located about a mile east of the station at Cross Creek Road. Allegedly, he was there to rob the place. The strange part was that he was wearing nothing but a Speedo. That attire would be unusual in most places, but this was a beach town, and people sometimes walked around like that. But to rob a bank?

A teller call the station "F.S. is here, and he's got a gun in his crotch," she said.

"Do you see the gun?" asked my friend Bob who was manning the desk that day. I was working as the jailer and listened in.

"No," she said, "but I know guns. I can see the shape of the gun in his Speedo."

She said she knew because her dad was a retired deputy, her sister was a deputy at Malibu, and she was dating a sergeant at the station. She had all the credentials to convince us that she knew what she was talking about.

Bob grabbed a shotgun and a radio car and tore over to Barclays. He needed to get the gun before people got hurt. Once he got there, he told the guy to put his hands in the air and not to move. He reached into the guy's Speedo to get the gun, and the guy climaxed all over Bob's hand.

He arrested F.S. on the charge of attempted bank robbery and brought him back to the station, and, man, was Bob hot, raging mad. He had a short fuse to start with. We all heard immediately about what happened in the bank. While we processed the suspect,

Bob was at a sink furiously washing his hands. I got on the P.A. and said, "Bob, F.S. says you're a stud, and he wants your home phone number, Big Boy."

Everyone at the station was crying from laughing so hard. I still can't tell that story without laughing. I don't know why no one knew that F.S. wasn't packing a gun. We had to let him go, but I'm sure it was a day Bob never forgot.

Saving Lives in Malibu

There are two events I will never forget from my time in Malibu. Both times, lives hung in the balance. The first was the blazing Clampitt and Wright Fires that swept through the canyons of Newhall and Malibu on Sept. 25, 1970, and merged to become the largest and deadliest wildfire in modern Los Angeles County history, up to that point.

The dry season in Southern California was always a dangerous time. Every year, there was the threat of fire sweeping over the ridges and into residential and business areas. The brush on the hills built up like kindling, and when the hot, dry Santa Ana winds blew, the hills could go up like a tinderbox. It was a recipe for disaster that has only gotten worse as more and more homes line the canyons where the Santa Ana winds blow. Fires in California have caused massive damage and loss of life and have made international news.

The Clampitt fire broke out around 8 a.m. that Friday, Sept. 25, near Clampitt Road in the Newhall Pass as a result of downed power lines. With winds clocking in at 80 mph, it took less than a day for the fire to make a 20-mile run to the coast, tearing through Porter Ranch, the Simi Hills at Chatsworth, south to the 101 Freeway and on to Malibu Canyon.

Thank goodness for Deputy Iman Mills. He had his act together and could handle crises. Truly, he was one of the finest, most professional deputies I ever knew. Before joining the force,

195

he had served twenty years in the Marines, a poster boy for them, and it showed. He has since passed away, I think from cancer. As soon as the fire started raging, Iman set up a chalkboard and coordinated all the people and notifications in our department. I was called in from my home in Camarillo. Everyone was called in to help evacuate people and keep them safe. Iman was so good he could have led whole armies into battle.

I remember hearing the report when the fire jumped the eight-lane 101 Freeway. It went by Whizin Market and came over the hills like a tidal wave, rushing all the way to the ocean, 10 miles within an hour and a half, destroying everything in its path. On the lookout for folks in trouble or who hadn't left their homes, I drove up to Trancas Canyon, north of the Malibu station. The smoke was so thick I couldn't see out of the windshield. Even the ice plant was burning. It looked like a war zone.

The 1970 Malibu fire.

Patrolling as fast as I could through the neighborhoods in a Ford Bronco, I came across a locked gate. Cars were parked on the other side and people stepped out of them and waved to me frantically. The home belonged to actor Paul Newman and because of the fire, there was no electricity to open the damn gate. They were trapped behind it. I wrapped a chain through the gate, connected it to the hitch on the Bronco, and pulled it down so they could escape. It's amazing what you can do in a crisis like that. You don't think; you just act.

The fire was moving so fast. Propane tanks were exploding left and right. It was pure chaos, like a scene out of hell. But the thing that sticks with me the most from that time was this poor horse that had gotten caught up in the fire and was badly burned. The owner took it to Zuma Beach, right across from Trancas, and asked one of the deputies to put it out of its misery. And the deputy did just that, right there on the beach. It was a mercy killing but a hard thing to witness.

We did what we could, but in the end, it was a reminder that nature is more powerful than us.

The second incident was sometime in 1971. I was patrolling up in Coral and Decker Canyon on one of the streets off the Pacific Coast Highway that take you into the hills west of Malibu Canyon. A lady was walking on the side of the road. As I drove closer, I could see blood dripping from her arm. I stopped, grabbed a towel from inside my car, and ran to her. The cut on her arm was sizable and looked self-inflicted, possibly an attempted suicide.

She was already kind of out of it from the blood loss and didn't respond to my questions. I think she was in shock. She couldn't tell me her name or where she lived. I have no idea how she got there, walking on the side of the road. I applied direct pressure with the towel and led her to my car, grabbing the radio through my open window with my other hand.

"101, 1033," I announced. My car number was 101. The code 1033 signals an emergency broadcast. "I have a nano two-way," I continued, "Request a two-man unit to meet me at Pacific Coast Highway for transportation to the hospital."

"10-4, 101," the dispatcher replied.

I guided the woman into the backseat of my car, showing her how to keep pressure on the wound, but she wouldn't do it. We sped down to the Pacific Coast Highway where a two-man car was waiting for me. I put her in their backseat. One of them sat in back with her to continue to apply the direct pressure she needed and, as she passed out, he started giving her mouth-to-mouth as they sped her off to the hospital in Santa Monica. She survived.

We had saved her life. Days like that made me feel like my work made a difference. I may not have done everything perfectly. I know I didn't. But I always wanted to do whatever I could to have a positive impact. That day, I felt like I had succeeded.

CHAPTER 15

Los Angeles County Detective, 1972–1975

A FTER MY TIME IN MALIBU, I transferred to the detectives unit at L.A. Metro headquarters. I was assigned to Lennox Station, located near the L.A. International Airport.

It was the start of very happy times for me personally. I married my third and final wife, the wonderful Dona, in 1973. My second marriage, lasting only through the time I was in Malibu, had deteriorated to the point of no return. She looked like Natalie Wood, a gorgeous gal, but we didn't get along. There were red flags from the beginning, but I wasn't paying enough attention, like the night we went to a Halloween party in Venice Beach while we were dating She got very flirtatious with some guy there I didn't even know, and she got drunk, very drunk. I was already not in the best of moods as I drove her home in my Porsche from the party in Venice to our place in Manhattan Beach. Then, she threw up all over the interior.

I never forgave her for that. That car was my baby. She repeatedly insulted my father. She hated my dad, who was an angel. You can't do that. You can't say bad things about someone's family. There was more. But it doesn't matter now. When I met Dona, we were off to the races.

Meeting the Woman of My Dreams

I actually met Dona through my second wife at a Christmas party for Toyota Motors on Century Boulevard in Beverly Hills, where they both worked. They were friends. That night, when I first saw Dona, I was with my second wife, and Dona was with her second husband. She wore a silver dress that effortlessly complimented her long dark hair and attractive figure and matched the sparkle in her eyes. She was entrancing. I didn't talk to her that night, but that vision of her stayed front and center in my mind. Soon after, we went on our first of several double dates, heading out to dinner in my Porsche, she and her husband crammed into the tiny backseat. I saw her every time I looked in the rearview mirror. I tried to ignore my feelings but couldn't stop glancing at her. It wasn't just her beauty. She was a bright light. I still said nothing, though. We were both married to other people. But by the third double date, she was glancing back at my reflection with a smile.

I saw her again at a birthday party for a friend of hers. We danced and chatted. We talked together so easily. It was clear that the attraction was mutual, and our connection was unusual and special. I'd never felt anything like it before.

A short time later, I decided my feelings for her were too big to ignore. I called her. We met at the Proud Bird, a famous restaurant on the approach landing to LAX. The big thing about the Proud Bird was that you could put headphones on and listen to the conversation between flight control in the tower and the pilots while they were landing. We never put our headphones on. Instead, we talked. The conversation became intense very quickly. "I'm not happy in my marriage. I hear you're not happy either," I said. She nodded. She allowed me to put my hand on her leg. The spark was instantaneous for both of us. We both went home wondering what to do, considering the consequences of different scenarios.

Several days later, just before Christmas, we met at a hotel for an afternoon tryst. We were together after that. She immediately told her husband she wanted a divorce, and on Christmas Day, I told my second wife. I didn't mean to have that conversation on Christmas Day. The plan was to get through the holidays first, but we were driving to my wife's folks' house when she said, "You want a divorce, don't you?" It was a direct question. I said yes. We didn't talk about it, but we were both fooling around on the side. It had never been solid with us. She was a gorgeous woman, but we weren't right together, and we both knew it.

With my beautiful wife, Dona.

In 1973, I sold my beloved Porsche to my volleyball partner—the end of an era—and Dona and I married in Reno, Nevada. It was just amazing, the most exciting time ever. With the money from the Porsche, we purchased a little house together in Manhattan Beach.

Dona and I had both been around the block. This was the third marriage for both of us, and it would be our last. She was the love of my life. When I married her, I said, "No complaining, no sniffling," more to myself than her. "We take care of each other. We put the other person first." She agreed wholeheartedly. I was so fortunate to find her.

Working with the DEA

Meanwhile, I started working undercover. During my days in uniform patrol, I made numerous drug arrests, mainly for marijuana, amphetamines and other pills, and heroin. Cocaine arrests also came within my scope when I became a detective. I made the most drug arrests of my career when I was working undercover. Among all the drugs, heroin was the worst I had to deal with. It was a killer. The situation is even more deadly today with fentanyl-laced drugs. Two milligrams can kill you. I never had to confront a drug as potent as that.

The heroin in Los Angeles, as in the rest of the country at that time, came mostly through the "French Connection," a collaboration between Corsican gangsters in Marseille and the Sicilian Mafia. You could tell the difference between their stuff, usually made from poppies grown in Afghanistan or Southeast Asia, and heroin from Mexico and South America. The Asian stuff was lighter in color. The stuff from South America was brown, and the tar heroin from Mexico resembled black licorice. It reminded me of an old breath freshener called Sen Sen. One reason why people overdose on heroin is due to the varying potency. The dealers get a kilo or a pound of pure heroin and cut it with lactose, a milk sugar.

They never want to sell pure heroin because that would be lethal, and their profits would dry up. So, they cut it with lactose, but since these people are not scientists, the concentration can range from 2 percent to 25 percent. No one knows what they're buying. It's that 25 percent stuff that can prove fatal, causing heroin overdoses. If a guy is used to a lower dosage and then gets slammed with an unexpectedly high dose, he ODs, and he's dead. That's how it works.

In 1973, I was assigned to work with the DEA involving a heroin case in Baldwin Hills. That neighborhood was home to high-end individuals like Ray Charles, Ike and Tina Turner, and Nancy Wilson. I was partnered up with Bill Hallick. Bill was an interesting character. He wasn't a big guy, maybe 5'10 and 160 pounds, but he had a presence. His father was from Samoa, and his mother was of German descent. His wife's name was Twinkles, and she was Hawaiian. Bill and I became really good friends, and later, he invited me to visit his family in Samoa, a story for later in this book.

As Bill and I embarked on this case, we collaborated with several DEA agents, most of whom were skilled professionals. I had a favorable impression of the DEA. I also held the U.S. Marshals in high regard, although my trust in the FBI was more selective from experience.

The DEA official in charge of the case was book smart, but he wasn't street-smart. I was working with about six other deputies and DEA agents who knew what they were doing. When the DEA agent laid out the plan, he said, "Okay, when we stop these cars that are purchasing drugs from the dealers, we'll move in and do our thing."

I immediately interjected, "Hold on a minute. Look at how we're dressed. Some of us look like homeless people. If we stop these guys, they might be carrying Roscoes"—that's street slang for hand guns. Rosco is a manufacturer of them. "If we stop them and they're armed, we might have a problem. They might think they're getting robbed." I proposed an alternative, "Let's have uniformed deputies carry out the stops." Luckily, the team leader listened, that's what they did, and it worked out. The arrests went down.

Although the DEA team couldn't locate the drugs they were originally searching for, I had an impressive success rate with search warrants, finding drugs in nearly 90% of the cases. I guess after enough experience, I had developed a knack for finding the drugs or was able to put myself into these guys' shoes and think like the dealers. I felt like a dope dog. On one occasion, we busted a dealer's house, and inside was a large stone fireplace made of river rock. Something caught my attention. I noticed a rock with no grout around it. My intuition kicked in, and I pulled it out, revealing a substantial quantity of hidden heroin.

A Dirty Job

I've been inside many houses you wouldn't want to enter, but there was one that was the worst I've ever seen. Trash was piled shoulder-high everywhere with walking paths through the trash leading from room to room. We were looking for the son of this family who was wanted for murder. I was with partners Don Scott and Charlie Martin. Charlie was an ex-Navy Seal, and Don was an ex-fighter. I was happy to be with such experienced guys because there was no telling what was lurking inside this house.

The kitchen was a disaster: rotted meat, animal waste, and dirty dishes and food packages everywhere. The smell was overwhelming. With every step, our shoes crunched, like we were stepping on sticks, but it was dead cockroaches. The weird thing was that the family that lived there had well-paying jobs. Yet they lived in absolute disgust. The mother said, "If I had more time, I would have cleaned the house for you." I said, "Madam, you don't have enough time in your life to clean this house. I'm going to call for an airstrike. We're going to eliminate it."

That house should have been condemned and burned to the ground. We all went outside and wiped our feet off on the grass to get the cockroach carcasses off the bottom of our shoes.

Cable Address—BANKAMERICA

Bank of America
NATIONAL TRUST ASSOCIATION

ROOM 705, 111 WEST SEVENTH STREET • LOS ANGELES, CALIFORNIA 90054

April 14, 1972

Peter J. Pitchess, Sheriff
Los Angeles County Sheriff's Department
Hall of Justice
211 West Temple Street
Los Angeles, Calif. 90012

Dear Sheriff Pitchess:

During the early part of this year, it came to the attention of Bank of America Special Agents and personnel of your department, that certain businessmen in and around the Lennox, Hawthorne and Hermosa Beach area, were involved in a large scale fraud operation in the use of credit cards. The dollar loss suffered by our company as well as other credit card companies was quite large, with the potential for additional loss reaching far greater amounts.

Sergeants Jack Dicus and Robert Laughlin were instrumental in spear-heading a very detailed and time consuming investigation, which culminated with the arrest of three persons responsible. Not only did these arrests stop existing Fraud from these sources, it prevented further expansion of these activities to other locations.

We are well aware of the numerous man hours spent on this investigation, and would like to thank your department for a tremendous job done. We know it would be impossible to thank all personnel involved in this matter, but would like to call to your attention those efforts expended by Sergeants Dicus and Laughlin and Deputies Lovette Caples, William Brauberger, Charles Martin, James Holland, Fred Bluett, Robert Mead, Steven Streaker, Fletcher Oliver and William Allen.

I would also like to take this opportunity to state that the response and co-operation extended by officers of your department has always been a source of major encouragement to Bank of America.

Best wishes for the continued success to you and members of your department, and if we can be of any assistance to you, please do not hesitate to call upon us.

Very truly yours,

James L. Swain
Assistant Vice President
Bank Security and Operating Loss Investigations

JLS:GL:wc

cc: Capt. Kenneth R. Hayes
     Capt. Victor Caballero
     Capt. Paul Strohman

As a detective, I tended to receive more commendations than before. It was always nice. This one was for a large-scale credit card fraud investigation, resulting in arrests.

The Mafia Professor

I had a snitch with whom I became pretty good friends over the years. He was not a made man, but he knew some influential people in organized crime. He explained to me how the Mafia laundered money. They would buy a business as a front, such as a restaurant, liquor store, or clothing store. They would fake bills of purchase—$200,000 for carpets and drapes and $50,000 for chairs and supplies—but none of those things were real. They didn't pay for them, and the items were never delivered. They were using the phony bills of purchase to launder illegal funds.

Then, they would bring out a guy from the east coast called The Professor. He was a member of the New York Mafia family. He would come out to these businesses, start a fire, and burn the evidence. They couldn't prove it was arson. He would do something with the wiring to make it look like an electrical short. He was very good at what he did and never got caught.

That's how the Mafia laundered millions of dollars. Then, they would file for the insurance on the business. It was all a way to game the system.

I wrote a memo on the information my snitch told me and gave it to my supervisors to share with New York PD. I hoped this intelligence was helpful to them.

Protection Duty

I've protected snitches, witnesses, actors and presidents. While working as a detective, I received orders to keep watch over a Spanish teacher at Morningside High School. Why? One of his previous jobs was as an assistant attorney general under Batista in Cuba. With Fidel Castro in charge, the attorney general in Cuba had just been assassinated, and our Sheriff believed others might be targeted. Our task felt like babysitting the man. But the instructions were clear: twelve-hour shifts with no days off for two weeks straight. Our shifts ran from 6:00 in the morning to 6:00 at night, while another crew took over from 6:00 at night to 6:00 in the morning. We told the teacher, "We're here for your protection and don't want anything to happen to you." Following the Sheriff's orders was akin to obeying a divine command. It's like God telling you. "Do it." If he said to do it, we did it. It left no room for hesitation.

During my time with the Spanish teacher, he shared with me that Batista had the opportunity to defeat Castro. However, Batista, being a crook more concerned with filling his pockets, failed to do what he had to. Consequently, Castro gained strength and popularity among the people, leading to the overthrow of the country's government. Then, of course, we almost had a nuclear confrontation because of that. Later, while traveling to Houston for an extradition, I met a Catholic priest who had defected from Cuba, and he said the same thing as the teacher from Morningside High School.

My fellow deputy, Joe Postell, was all smiles when he told me about his protection duty. He was ordered to pick up someone at the airport and take him home. It turned out to be Kareem Abdul-Jabbar. His team, the Milwaukee Bucks were in L.A. to play the Lakers. Perhaps the greatest center ever to play basketball, Rookie-of the-Year in his first season with the Bucks, the league's Most Valuable Player during the next two seasons, he asked to play in the 1973 All-Star game, his fourth All-Star game in as many pro seasons, but he declined. Instead, he attended the funeral of seven people murdered in a horrible attack on a building he owned in Washington, D.C. Four children were drowned in the attack. It was one of the most heinous crimes of the era and the largest mass killing in Washington, D.C. Prior to that, Abdul-Jabbar was among several top collegiate players who had declined to play for the U.S. basketball team in the 1968 Olympics with comments that are similar to that of former NFL player Colin Kaepernick about white privilege, racism, and violence against blacks.

When Abdul-Jabbar played in the 1973 season, police were often stationed at both ends of his corridor in the team hotel. Security guards lined the court during practices and games. Wayne Embry, Milwaukee Bucks general manager, was quoted as saying, "It was no joking matter,. Nobody wanted to sit next to him on the bench. There were constant threats. It was a rough time, extra security around the court wherever we played. It was pretty tense."

Joe Postell met Abdul at the airport to take him to where he was staying in Los Angeles. He was pretty excited and determined to give the basketball player, whom he admired for both his beliefs and his athletic accomplishments, as much anonymity and security as possible, so he drove him in his personal vehicle. The problem was it was a V.W. Bug. Kareem is seven-two! His knees were up to his chin as he sat in Joe's car. That was funny.

Strange Cases in Lennox

There were always more than a few strange cases in every phase of my career. There was a man who lived near Lennox Station who raised parakeets. He kept the birds in an outdoor cage. One night, he heard them squawking, just going crazy. He went outside to investigate to find an unknown man inside the cage, biting off the heads of the parakeets and dropping the bodies on the ground. The birds couldn't escape. He called us and we responded in time to catch the perpetrator in the act. The guy got put away on 5150 psychiatric. I don't think there was any question that he needed to be off the streets.

The strangest court case I ever witnessed was in Inglewood. Four women were victims of the crime, but I only heard one woman testify. The suspect was an ex-University of Oregon student. He took medical classes, so he knew medical terms, but he didn't finish his Oregon degree and instead returned to his family home in South L.A. Something was wrong with the young man. He called these women with crazy stories and instructions. The woman I heard testify said he called her saying, "I'm Dr. Jolan from Harbor General Hospital," which was near San Pedro. "Mrs. Jones, your husband was in an automobile accident, and his private area has been crushed. We have to operate on him, and we need you to get him sexually stimulated. So, I want you to go outside, find the first man you see, take him into your house, have sex with him, and explain what's going on on the phone so we can get him through this operation." She was a very naive gal. She actually went outside to look, went back inside and said to this supposed doctor on the phone, "Doctor, I can't find anyone."

He was convicted on four charges of fraud and sentenced to two years in the county jail. I know I said it before, but it bears repeating" there are some strange people out there.

Defense Attorneys Running Wild

I know someone has to do it, but given my experiences in court, I'm not a big fan of defense attorneys. We had a saying: "Sharks and attorneys are exactly alike, except sharks don't eat attorneys as a professional courtesy." Some of them were just doing their jobs and were okay, but I witnessed too many playing dirty to get their clients off. We worked hard to bust these guys, and these attorneys pulled every trick in the book to get them back on the street, even when it was clear that the suspects were guilty. They would tell the judge things like, "My client is no longer a sexual predator. He's cured of his problem and should be freed and released on bail." These attorneys weren't doing it for justice. They were doing it for money. I always wished the judge would say something like, "Okay, counselor, if we free him, he gets to spend six months at your house babysitting your kids since he's cured of his sexual deviancy."

One example of shark defense was for a robbery and assault with a deadly weapon, a 245 PC. When we arrived on the scene, this guy who owned this Mom and Pop store was lying on the ground behind the counter. He was about eighty and had been pistol-whipped, kidnapped, tied up, and robbed. We located the suspect and booked him for a robbery, kidnapping, and assault with a deadly weapon. The case went to court. The victim was not in good health. According to California criminal law, the defense attorney knew that if the victim died, the court would be forced to decide that no crime had been committed, because there would be no victim, especially if the elderly victim died of "natural causes." So, the defense attorney asked for a continuance. He wanted to run out the clock on this eighty-year-old store owner to keep his scumbag client out of jail.

I went to the judge and said, "Your Honor, let me tell you, this guy is trying to get a continuance because he wants the victim to die, so there'll be no case." I said, "He's going to continue it and continue it."

The judge told the suspect and his attorney, "If I give you a continuance, here's what's going to happen: if you're found guilty, I will sentence you on the robbery, the kidnapping, and assault with a deadly weapon and make all three charges run consecutively, which means when you finish the robbery beef, you do the kidnapping beef, then you do assault with a deadly weapon time. Right now, if you take the deal the prosecutor is offering, the sentence runs concurrently, all at the same time. What you're doing to manipulate this case and run out the clock on the victim's life is called "running wild." If you're going to play chicken, let's see who wins." So, the guy pleaded guilty. The judge sentenced him to three concurrent sentences. I was pleased to be a part of that justice.

INTERPOL

On one occasion as a detective, I worked indirectly with INTERPOL, the International Criminal Police Organization. INTERPOL is an intergovernmental organization with 195 cooperating nations. If you are the victim of a crime committed by someone from another country, INTERPOL steps in and networks police and experts to catch the assailant. I had only heard the name before and didn't know much about the organization. A fellow detective and I were sent to interview a woman in Marina Del Rey, a very striking flight attendant for American Airlines. In those days, we still called them "stewardesses" (my wife Dona was one). They were almost all women and wore uniforms of heels and skirts—short skirts in the 1970s. Joking around with other guys, we sometimes call them "hostitutes." It was a different day and age. I'd never do that now; I'd get in trouble! The woman was working on a flight to Finland, and from there, she and another flight attendant took a train to St. Petersburg, Russia, to do a little sightseeing. According to the report I had, she and her companion were in a sleeper car when a drunken Russian soldier barged in and accosted her. The soldier was arrested for attempted rape. Our job was to get the story from the victim for the criminal case in the Russian courts.

The woman shook her head. "The guy was just drunk. He didn't try to rape me or anything like that. It was nothing. He didn't grab me, attack me, or try to rip my clothes off. He shouldn't have been arrested for that."

We wrote our report, turned it into headquarters, and they sent it to INTERPOL. That was my only contact with INTERPOL in all my police actions, so I wasn't able to get an impression of the organization, but I would've liked to get to know that force more and what they were like.

Fugitive Detail

For a while I worked on the Fugitive Detail, which was a part of the detective unit. Our job was to track down and capture suspects on the run, even if they fled to L.A. from elsewhere and to transport inmates to other states or foreign countries for trial. We flew and drove all over the United States to deliver these guys.

In one case, a suspect who had been arrested in Salt Lake City, refused to fly back to L.A. He claimed to be afraid of flying, so we had to transport him back by ground. This suspect was trained in martial arts, so we had to be careful. Sergeant Tommy Johnson and Dennis Lobes, a deputy I had never met before, accompanied me. Now, Dennis was quite the character. He had gone to Japan to study karate and achieved a fifth-degree black belt. Despite being a skinny little guy, he was not to be underestimated. He knew how to take care of business. We flew to Salt Lake City to pick up the suspect and brought him back to L.A. Dennis told lots of stories about his karate fights so the suspect would understand what he was up against if he tried anything.

We flew all over the country on Fugitive Detail. Some guys even flew to foreign countries. I knew two guys who flew to Italy to return a very big embezzler. I did fugitive runs to Albuquerque, Dallas and Houston. We transported suspects on commercial airplanes, but the FAA wouldn't let us handcuff them on the plane. It would upset the other passengers. We just had to stay very aware and right next to our fugitives during the flight. If they had to go to the bathroom, we escorted them and stood outside. And we had a trick up our sleeves for loading them on and off the planes in the airports when we couldn't have them in cuffs. We attached a long surgical metal strip to the fugitive's leg with a little hasp by the knee. This allowed the fugitive to bend his knee to sit, but if the guy tried to run, the hasp would cause his leg to straighten out. It would have been easy to catch a guy if he decided to run.

We always had to be on high alert. We were the first ones on the plane and the first ones off. And we were always carrying guns, even on commercial flights. We had at least two deputies in plain clothes if we were transporting a dangerous suspect.

Transporting fugitives always carried an element of danger. I remember one case where a uniformed, married deputy was fired and tried in court for having sex with minors who were part of the Explorer program, which was for teenagers, boys and girls, who wanted to become police officers. When a girl came forward, he turned himself in at his local station.

It was my job to drive him to the county jail to be booked for his crimes. The sergeant in charge said, because this guy had been a deputy, "Let's cuff him in the front." Big mistake. I don't care if he's Mother Theresa; you always handcuff a suspect in the back. I could see the deputy in the mirror on the freeway. He looked me in the eyes and said, "If I was a bad guy, I could kill you right now." If he had a loaded gun hidden in his crotch, he could have pulled it out and taken us down. It was just a reminder that one mistake in our line of work could get you killed.

Losing Dale

This story is very close to my heart and still hurts to this day because I was there; I witnessed the whole thing, and I lost a friend.

I had become the senior officer of the Fugitive Detail, and my boss was Dale Wyman, a sharp guy with a Type A personality, a work hard-play hard kind of guy, very detail-oriented, a very good officer. Unfortunately, he suffered from PTSD, stressed and anxious ever since killing someone in a shooting a few years before. He smoked and drank a lot.

We were finishing the paperwork on a case in the office, and he complained that he had a bad headache. I gave him a couple of Excedrin that I had on me, and as we parted at the end of the day, we decided to meet up in the San Fernando Valley the next day for breakfast on our way to work.

The next morning at Carrows, Dale was late, which was very unusual. He was always on time. I ordered my coffee and waited. He finally arrived, looking concerned and not well. His face was pale. "Bob, I'm seeing visions of three," he told me. He ordered coffee. I started to ask him questions, but a moment later he said, "My vision is getting cloudy." I asked if he wanted to go to the hospital. He shook his head. Another minute later, he grabbed my arm, "I can't see at all. Bob, I can't see."

He still insisted on not going to the hospital. He wanted to go home. I called the office on the handheld radio to report Dale's condition and tell them that I was taking the officer, Mr. Wyman, home. I helped him to bed, told his wife everything, and went to the office, where I explained what had happened in more detail.

When I checked in the next day, his wife told me that Dale ended up being ambulanced to the hospital after all. He had a brain stem stroke, which is the worst kind. He lost the use of his arms, legs, and just about everything. He was just a hunk of meat with a heart, and that was all. The only thing he could do was open his eyes. It was just tragic. They weren't up for visitors until about six weeks later. I went to visit him, along with two other deputies, at a recovery hospital in Pasadena. We wanted to give him a laugh, anything, so we told him we would get a nurse to give him a blow job. His eyes got really big. Of course, we were only joking; his wife was right there in the hallway.

Dale never recovered. He held on for quite a while in that state and died about twelve years later. At that time, L.A. County didn't cover strokes as a disability. It was not in the county code. After about six months, Dale's family had to file a claim in Superior Court asking for enough money for his care. I testified about the circumstances of his situation, what happened, his demeanor, how he lost his sight, everything. The county ruled in his favor and granted him a full retirement, a million dollars for the special care he needed, and a van designed for folks with physical disabilities, with ramps, and handholds so his family could transport him when needed.

I never saw him after that last day in Pasadena, although I checked in about him with his son, a sergeant and my supervisor, when I moved on to work with the U. S. Marshals. I still think about Dale from time to time.

LOS ANGELES POLICE DEPARTMENT

EDWARD M. DAVIS
Chief of Police

Mailing Address: Box 30158
Los Angeles, Calif. 90030

Ref. No. 6.4.2

TOM BRADLEY
Mayor

January 15, 1974

Captain Victor J. Cavallero
Commander, Metropolitan Bureau
Los Angeles County Sheriff's Office
1625 West Olympic Boulevard, Room 905
Los Angeles, California 90015

Dear Captain Cavallero:

Please accept our thanks and appreciation for the valuable
assistance extended by your Metro Bureau, and most notably
Metro Bureau, Lennox Station, in the arrest of Elvin Ivan
Edwards, Booking No. 2726-443, of 2217 South Hobart Boulevard,
#3, Los Angeles, for 496 P.C.

Information developed by Sergeant A. Lamensdorf and his team
members was instrumental in providing essential information
needed by this Investigative Division to complete our grand theft
investigation under DR 73-692 055. Victim--Desmond's Department
Store, 4145 South Crenshaw Boulevard, Los Angeles. Property
recovered as a result of this arrest is estimated at approximately
$150,000.

Sergeant Lamensdorf and his team members, during the course of
the investigation, demonstrated a degree of professionalism
commensurate with the high standards of your Department. Again,
many thanks for your cooperation in this joint venture.

Very truly yours,

E. M. DAVIS
Chief of Police

T. D. Haire

T. D. HAIRE, Captain
Commanding Officer
Wilshire Investigative Division

cc: Captain K. Hays

This commendation was for helping the LAPD find a grand theft auto suspect.

215

PETER J. PITCHESS, SHERIFF

County of Los Angeles

Office of the Sheriff

Hall of Justice

Los Angeles, California 90012

February 3, 1975

Deputy Robert G. Mead
425 - 36th Street
Manhatten Beach, California 90266

Dear Deputy Mead:

I have been informed that you have recently completed a
major milestone in your career with this Department, fifteen
years of service. You and your many fellow employees, through
diligent service and devotion to duty, have made the Department
of the Sheriff an organization of which we can all be proud.

Your Unit Commander will present you with a service pin com-
memorating your achievement. Please accept this pin and my
personal congratulations for fifteen years of dedication to
the County and this Department.

Sincerely,

PETER J. PITCHESS
SHERIFF

Fifteen years had gone by!

CHAPTER 16

Working with the U.S. Marshals, 1975

I HAVE A LETTER STATING I WAS A MEMBER of the U.S. Marshals for two weeks. The L.A. Sheriff's Department was part of this huge statewide operation in the "war on drugs." The Bureau of Narcotics and Dangerous Drugs was founded under the Johnson administration in 1968 to deal with the rise in recreational drug use and import of narcotics, but the war on drugs became official at a press conference in 1971 when President Nixon named drug abuse as "public enemy number one in the United States." In 1973 he set up the "super agency," the Drug Enforcement Administration, to handle all aspects of the drug problem in the country. Heroin and cocaine especially were leading to addiction and crime.

We were brought into the operation because, as locals, we knew the local territory better than anybody. They needed us. The U.S. Marshal's office provided the federal financing and the cars. They also partnered with LAPD and other police and sheriff offices all over California, from San Diego to Sacramento and even farther north. It was a very expensive operation resulting in over 3,000 arrests, all felonies. And no one got shot. The culminating event was the arrest of a major dope dealer in Northern California.

The Feds seized his mansion and estate, which were worth over 25 million dollars. It paid for the whole operation when everything was sold, so it didn't cost the taxpayers any money. That was handled well.

I was called in again to work with the U.S. Marshals the next year, this time in my capacity as a detective for the LASD. Our chief of detectives asked eight of us to work with them. We were assigned to pick up fugitives statewide. We had a long list of 2,160 fugitives, all for felonies. We were supposed to bring in as many on the list as possible. For the next eight weeks, that's what we did. Our jurisdiction was all of Southern California, from San Diego to L.A.

We headquartered the operation at a Marine recruiting office in Pico Rivera. I lived in Camarillo at the time, which made for a sixty-seven mile commute each way. I worked from six in the morning to six at night for eight weeks. Sometimes, we worked until eight o'clock at night, and I'd get home at ten. To make it by six a.m., I'd have to get up at four in the morning to drive to Pico, but I was never late. I was never late to the job in twenty-nine years.

I was paired up with a U.S. Marshal named Thomas Lopez, a really good dude. All the guys in the Marshal's office were really good people. We had to get creative to apprehend some of these fugitives. If they had evaded law enforcement before, we needed to think up ways to bring them in without creating a dangerous situation. We made our two best arrests using the postal service.

We were looking for this one guy who said he was a doctor and was wanted for murdering a prostitute. He had picked up the hooker and asked her to give him oral sex while he was driving. She wouldn't do it, so he put a gun to her head, opened the door of his car while it was speeding down the freeway and kicked her out while the car was moving and she died. These were the types of wonderful people we had to find and get off the streets.

It took us nearly a week to get him. First, we had to track him down, which wasn't easy. In so doing, we discovered he had a mailbox at the post office in West L.A. We followed his movements and finally one day waited for him inside the post office, staying out of sight by hanging out where the postal workers stuffed the boxes. When we saw his mail being pulled out of the box from the other side, we ran out to the front area and surrounded him, putting a gun in each of his ears. His eyes went wide in surprise. We put the cuffs on him, read him his rights, and hauled him to jail.

When I think about it, our funniest arrest was Elvin Flanagan, a Black guy with an Irish name, unusual at the time, wanted on a robbery charge. First, we went to Flanagan's house. He wasn't home, so I told the woman who answered the door, "I've got a package for Mr. Flanagan. When's he going to be back?"

"He'll be back later," she said

"Here's a card. Call me. We'll get the package to him."

The phone number was a cold line set up to catch guys who thought they were getting a package. When any of us answered that line, we didn't say "U.S. Marshals." We said, "Package delivery."

Elvin had no idea what was going on, and he called us. He said, "I'm going to be home in twenty minutes." We sent the delivery truck over, and Elvin ran right outside from his house, right to the truck. He didn't know what he was going to get, but he ran out like a kid on Christmas to get the package we had promised. Thomas Lopez and I were in an undercover car behind the truck. We got out, and, once again, put a gun in each of his ears. We liked to do it like that, the gun-in-the-ear trick. It really got the suspect's attention. I had to try hard not to laugh as his eyes went wide.

Elvin wasn't too smart. I might even say he had the brain of a chicken. Even as we were putting him in handcuffs, he still hadn't figured out he'd been tricked. He said, "Where's my motherfucking package?" He still had no idea what was happening to him.

We continued to work the fugitive list until we got all the bad guys listed off the streets. Sometimes, they had no idea we were coming for them. Whenever we caught one of these guys, checking them off the list felt fulfilling. It was even better when we used a creative way to catch them. It made for great stories too.

On The FBI

I enjoyed working with the U.S. Marshals. I also worked with ATF, DEA, and even the Secret Service a little bit. But working with the FBI, I grew to distrust them. Many of them were good enough guys and smart—when I lived in Camarillo, a few of my neighbors were FBI agents. They could write reports, sure. They could do investigations.

Delivering a "package" undercover

They were paid a lot of money for the big cases, and they had fewer restrictions than we did, so they could plant bugs where local law enforcement couldn't. In general, they had expertise in fingerprints and recordings. Financial restraints hampered local law enforcement agencies, but not the FBI. But none of them had any street training. The FBI didn't understand "bad guys." They couldn't do their job without paid snitches. The Feds didn't work the streets; they didn't talk to everyday people. They didn't break up bar fights. They weren't involved in armed stand-offs, except for the guys on their SWAT team. They paid other people to do their work. They used the expertise of local law enforcement and took the credit.

The other issue with the FBI was a culture of taking care of number one. They lacked the essential ethic in law enforcement that we take care of one another, first and foremost. In our sheriff's department, you never let your partner down. You protect and support each other. Not the FBI. You make a mistake on a report or drink too much with the boys in your off-hours—not on duty—the Feds would snitch you off in a heartbeat, especially if they thought it could get them a promotion. I saw a lot of self-aggrandizement. People talked about their colleagues behind their backs, except their director. Until he died in 1972, no one was taking potshots at J. Edgar Hoover, because the man was too powerful and had people behind him protecting his dirty activities. After he died, they started ragging on their old boss about his lifestyle and everything he did.

Even now, I don't trust the FBI. From what I see, playing politics still gets in the way of them doing their jobs. Money and promotions still seem to rule the department.

CHAPTER 17

Los Angeles County Detective Continued 1975–1984

Infiltrating Posse Comitatus

I N 1975, I WENT UNDERCOVER IN SACRAMENTO to investigate a far right-wing group called Posse Comitatus. It was one of the most fascinating and dangerous cases I worked as a detective. With a survivalist stance, these nutballs had loosely formed their own militia. The group was made of a bunch of conspiracy-minded, anti-government, anti-Semitic, white Christian supremacists. And we had to pretend we belonged in order to gather information about the Posse and find out all we could about their movements, plans, and who was in the group. These guys made a lot of threats and talked about assassinating judges and D.A.s.

These guys took their name from the Posse Comitatus Act, a law enacted in 1878 that bars federal troops from participating in civilian law enforcement except when expressly authorized by law. For these guys that law embodied an "American tradition" that sees military interference in civilian affairs as a threat to both democracy and personal liberty. In Latin, Posse Comitatus means "force of the county." They didn't believe in paying taxes or getting driver's licenses. They had chapters all around the country.

Undercover in plain clothes and in an unmarked car

I had great partners for the assignment: one of the best cops I ever knew, Steve Simone, who worked for the Montebello Police Department as a lieutenant and later became a chief; and a Homicide detective named Mike Robinson.

Our tech unit made us fake IDs for the job. I had a fake Social Security number and all of the supporting documents for a new identity. That's when I used the name Wayne Collins. The head of our tech squad was brilliant. He developed the voice print technology they used in the '70s. He could build cars and engines and was kind enough to build my first computer in 1971. He was like Q in the James Bond movies.

Steve, Mike and I drove up to Sacramento, working in plain clothes and an undercover car. I had long hair to fit in better. We didn't have a master plan; we went in cold, for the most part, staying at a Holiday Inn.

The next day we entered this big meeting room containing about a hundred people all carrying guns and knives and talking about killing people. As far as I know, they may or may not have committed

A souvenir from the undercover assignment with the Posse Comitatus.

any crimes before, but these guys were boasting about what they wanted to do. We had left our guns in the trunk of our car, which only made the situation more unnerving. We were in there without any protection. It was just the first of three days on the job, the length of the "conference."

But we had Steve Simone. Steve was so good he could've talk me into a sex change! Charismatic as hell, he made everything sound great. When Steve went into the Posse Comitatus meeting, it was like the Second Coming. They loved him. He started talking to people, and after about an hour, they elected him secretary. Afterwards, we had a good laugh about that. His position yielded great results for us. When the meeting was over, we had all these fools' names and addresses, which we included in our report. I think this helped in 1978 when the Posse tried to take over all of Alpine County in California. They wanted to create their own sovereign state.

I learned a lot from the many great people I worked with over the years. Steve was one of them. We often had to use our wits to get bad guys to comply with our wishes. We couldn't always walk into a location with our guns out and take everyone down, nor did we want to. If we could talk them down by being a bit crafty, that was a better option.

The Mexican Mafia

Arresting high-level gang members is no joke.

We had a prison gang unit that would go to the prisons and talk to the prisoners, just talk, quietly, gaining their trust and information. These officers were an important part of our surveillance team that helped put many sting operations into action. The gang members in the prisons didn't know they were snitching out their fellow gang members. With their work, we had the evidence we needed to arrest suspects and accomplices on the outside. This was true of a Mexican Mafia leader we went after in 1978.

To this day, the Mexican Mafia is considered the deadliest and most powerful gang in the California prison system with about 400 members and an estimate of more than 50,000 foot soldiers who carry out the gang's illegal activities on the streets in the hopes of becoming full members. Gang bangers.

The Mexican Mafia was formed in 1957 by Los Angeles street gang members incarcerated in a California Youth Authority facility.

We got a tip on the location of gang members who had been robbing banks. It was a fairly large operation. We used undercover cars and a camper truck for our stake out. My partner, Jim Callit, and I got into the back of the camper while another undercover cop drove. Other plain clothes detectives were in unmarked cars accompanying us. Over our radios, we had to talk in a code we created for the bust, figuring that they could always be listening to us on with radio scanners. We parked the camper truck a hundred yards from the suspect's house where we could do our surveillance. Our driver got out and joined his partner in one of the cars, which was parked about two hundred yards away in one direction. We had another car waiting on the road in the other direction.

Jim Callit and I sat in the back of the camper and took turns watching the house, so we always had eyes on it. Jim snacked on pickled pig's feet, grease running down his hands. I ate sunflower

ROCK - STONE	= Suspect or subsequent suspects i.d.'d by number.
ROCKS IN	= Suspect in Sock.
ROCKS OUT	= Suspect out of Sock. (Ex: Rocks out stage #)
ROCKS TENDING	= Suspect intending to (Ex: Rocks tending right Beverly)
STAGE	= Location or subsequent location i.d.'d by number.
STAGE CHECK	= Obtain residence location and description.
SOCK	= Vehicle or subsequent vehicles i.d.'d by number
SOCK 25	= Suspicious vehicle/look out for vehicle
SOCK CHECK	= Get License number and all particulars on vehicle.
BOX	= Street block.
LOT	= Parking lot (Ex: Rocks stored lot Willie)
ACTING	= Moving (Ex: Rocks acting)
FOOT	= Suspect on foot (Ex: Rocks foot Willie)
STORED	= Stopped (Ex: Rocks stored) Parked
CHARLIE	= Crossing or passing intersection. (Ex: Rock Charlie Slauson)
ADAM/POCHING	= Approaching (Ex: Rocks Adam Slauson)
TAR	= Taking off or On Ramp. (Ex: Rocks Tar #605)
ROSE/RUBY	= Has red light. (Ex: Rocks Rose or Ruby)
KELLY/EMERALD	= Has Greenlight. (Ex: Rocks Emerald or Kelly)
ROCKS IN #___	= Lane that suspect is in. (Ex: Rocks in #1/Rocks in #1 tending left)
FORWARD	= Suspect vehicle ahead of point vehicle. (Ex: Rocks forward 3)
CHASE	= Vehicle attempting to locate subject (Residential Area) Ex: 288 Chase
SET	= Point vehicle or unit with point on home or unit in position.
STASH	= Immediate pull-over into driveway, make turn, etc.
CHECK	= All surveillance units hit tail lights 3 or 4 times in order to locate all vehicles.
SPREADER	= Spread it out - Unit(s) too close.
CLOSE IT	= Close units up re: heavy traffic, etc.
TRANSFER	= Change point.
JAM	= Converge on suspect.

This was the terminology we used when chasing the Mexican Mafia and other prison gangsters on the streets because they often had scanners that infiltrated our car radios.

seeds. When the suspect left his house, we got on the radio, "The rock is in the sock. He's north on the major in a #6," meaning a Chevy. The undercover cars jammed him so he couldn't move his car and arrested him at gunpoint. With this method, my partner and I, as part of a team of seven deputies, arrested four Mexican Mafia guys for thirty bank robberies, and the FBI recognized us for it. There were no shootings. No one got hurt. It went very smoothly.

Entering a Home for an Arrest

Sometimes, we didn't get so lucky to be able to wait for the bad guys to come out and get arrested. Sometimes, we had to make contact or enter a building to make something happen. It was always dangerous to go into a house to nab a suspect, but sometimes we had know other choices. For example, if somebody stayed in a house for a couple of days while we sat in our cars waiting, at that point, it was time to put on costumes, ones that elicited enough trust to get them to open the front door to us. My favorite costume was a Catholic priest. My partner and I traded off wearing that one. Whoever was in the alb knocked on the door, and said, "Hi, I'm Father Jones. You're under arrest."

One home arrest that comes to mind was a heroin case, a buy-bust in El Segundo. A buy-bust is when an undercover officer makes a buy from a dealer and signals to the officers watching that the sale has been made. The signal puts the officers in motion, and they bust the dealer.

Several of us were surrounding the house of the dealer armed and ready. When we got the signal from the undercover officer that the buy had been made from a heroin dealer, I went around to kick in the back door with a uniformed officer. The doorjamb broke at the hinge to allow entry. We saw the suspect in the kitchen. The El Segundo PD officer with me told him once, twice and then a third time to drop his gun. Thankfully, he did after the third command,

UNITED STATES DEPARTMENT OF JUSTICE

FEDERAL BUREAU OF INVESTIGATION
11000 Wilshire Boulevard
Los Angeles, California 90024
April 28, 1978

In Reply, Please Refer to
File No.

Sheriff Peter J. Pitchess
Los Angeles County Sheriff's Office
Hall of Justice, Room 266
211 West Temple Street
Los Angeles, California 90012

Dear Sheriff Pitchess:

I wish to commend through you the exemplary efforts of seven members of your department who are currently assigned to the Prison Gang Task Force Surveillance Unit. The investigative persistence and thoroughness of these men have been responsible for the identification and/or apprehension of three armed Los Angeles bank robbers during the past three months.

These suspects, John Gilbert Quinones, Benito Rodriguez Arzaga, and John Thomas Lopez were believed to be involved separately in nearly 30 bank robberies in Los Angeles and Orange Counties.

The following members of your department have consistently displayed those high professional standards demanded of all members of your department, and are a credit to our law enforcement community:

Deputy Art Morales   Deputy Jim Catlett
Deputy Lou Saggiani   Deputy Robert Mead
Deputy Leonard Flores   Deputy Leroy Boyd
Deputy Lee Jackson

Very truly yours,

TED L. GUNDERSON
Special Agent in Charge

By: *David H. Cook*
DAVID H. COOK
Supervisory Special Agent

Accommodations from the FBI to the seven of us for capturing the suspects of the bank robberies.

76 1 551 N25 SH-AD-32 8/63

COUNTY OF LOS ANGELES

SHERIFF'S DEPARTMENT

DATE October 3, 1974

OFFICE CORRESPONDENCE

FILE NO.

FROM: R. A. Rodriguez, Captain
Major Crimes Bureau

TO: V. J. Cavellero, Captain
Metropolitan Bureau

SUBJECT: COMMENDABLE CONDUCT OF METROPOLITAN BUREAU PERSONNEL
DURING LAKEWOOD STATION ROBBERY SURVEILLANCE OPERATION
SEPTEMBER 26, 1974 THROUGH SEPTEMBER 29, 1974

Lieutenant Stuart Hansell, #37294	Deputy Jack Hughes, #43268
Sergeant Bob Briley, #10164	Deputy Buddy Lewis, #53480
Sergeant Arthur Lamensdorf, #51639	Deputy Charles Martin, #57660
Sergeant Frank Linley, #54112	Deputy John Martin, #57712
Sergeant Reynold Verdugo, #93469	Deputy Robert Mead, #61157
Deputy Lester Boal, #07950	Deputy Griffith Morrison, #64618
Deputy Carlos Bowers, #09007	Deputy John Ober, #67556
Deputy Vernon Clover, #06530	Deputy Robert Puente, #73499
Deputy Lance Galletch, #31448	Deputy Michael Roche, #77225
Deputy Robert Hogaboam, #41453	Deputy Donald Scott, #81019

In September 1974, a series of small business robberies began in the
Lakewood Station area which were jointly investigated by Robbery Detail
and Lakewood Station detectives. By September 25, 1974, the same two
suspects had committed a total of eight armed robberies.

Due to the frequency and pattern, the suspects had developed in these
robberies, a surveillance was initiated by Robbery Detail with the
cooperation of the Metropolitan Bureau.

Without exception, the above Metropolitan Bureau personnel, displayed
initiative, imagination and expertise in their conduct during the
surveillance operation. The demonstrated ability of these alert
Deputies, is a reflection on their training and desire to perform in
an outstanding manner in any given situation.

On September 29, 1974, at 2130 hours, one of the suspects committed
a robbery of a gas station within the surveillance area and all the
units upon receiving the robbery information proceeded to positions
within the area attempting to observe the suspect in his flight. At
2145 hours, Sergeant Lamensdorf and Deputy Scott observed the suspect
vehicle with the suspect driving.

Another surveillance job

because if he didn't, I had a twelve-gauge shotgun in my hand, and
I might've had to dust the guy, blow him out of his socks before he
shot one of us.

During that arrest, and any arrest with drugs, you yell, "No one
moves!" And I make sure they don't, not bystanders and certainly

229

not the suspect. I don't care if they have to go to the bathroom or the kettle is whistling on the stove. You never know when someone has firearms stashed somewhere.

Besides the dealer, there was a woman with a ten-month-old baby. She said, "Let me just change the baby's diaper. His diapers are in the next room."

"No, ma'am. No one moves," I said. Soon, we had arresting officers and child support services there to take all the suspects away. Once they were gone, we searched the house. I found a loaded .357 Magnum handgun among the diapers in the next room. There was also heroin and a FIT kit in the woman's purse. That's a junkie's outfit, her drug accessories: a syringe, a spoon, and a tie-off to pump the vein. If we had let her "change the baby's diaper," I'm pretty sure she would've killed us.

We arrested everyone involved, and they went to jail for the sale of heroin. When we went to court in South Bay Torrance for the preliminary hearing, the woman's attorney, a public defender, called me a liar. That PD would have defended Satan if she had to. I knew the judge on the case, Bernard Waller. They called him State Prison Waller because he put a lot of people away. I was really pissed off that she called me a liar, so I put my thumbnail to my tooth and flicked my wrist at her. In Italian, that means fuck you. I shouldn't have done that in court, but the judge ignored my actions. He knew I was telling the truth.

Getting a Fugitive to Come Outside

We got really lucky with this one bad guy, wanted for robbery. He lived in an apartment in South L.A., in the Culver City area. He was known to carry a gun, and we didn't want any problems. We didn't want a hostage situation. We knew what kind of car he had, so I called him and said, "Hey, I live near you. I was pulling my car out of the carport, and I dented the side of your car. I want to make it right. I'm an honest guy and want to take care of it. I'm sorry."

The guy fell for it. He came out in his bathrobe, and we arrested him. That was fun.

Once a Murderer, Always

It became very clear early on patrolling the streets how little people actually understand how the law works, and in particular, the statute of limitations. Some suspects just thought they could run away and get ahead of any charges they had hanging over their heads. There was a murder in Alabama in the 1940s. Law enforcement there had proof of who committed the crime and the perpetrator's fingerprints on file, but fingerprints weren't computerized like they are now. They were just in a manila file folder in Alabama until the FBI began using the Automated Fingerprint Identification System (AFIS) in 1974. To make storing and sharing fingerprints easier among law enforcement agencies, AFIS, developed by third party vendors, computerized the fingerprint card system. It made a big difference when it came to finding fugitives.

The suspect, unbeknownst to anyone, had moved to L.A. from Alabama. I arrested him for drunk driving one night, not knowing who he was, until we booked him, and his fingerprints matched those of a murder suspect who had killed someone thirty years before. There's no statute of limitations on murder, so we booked him for the crime. He had been driving drunk with his family in the car—really stupid and irresponsible—so they were all there at the station. It was a sad scene. His kids were crying; his wife was crying—they didn't know anything about his past. He was transported back to Alabama to stand trial. I have a commendation from the Alabama Department of State Police for my work on that case.

Improving Station Security

I tried to make things better for people. I sincerely wanted to keep good people safe. I like helping others. I was always on the lookout for ways to improve things at the station and keep my colleagues as safe as possible since it was already tough being a sheriff's deputy. There was a shooting at the LAPD Hollywood station, where a citizen walked in the back door with a raised gun. The officers killed him inside the station. That made me realize that security was lax at every station in L.A., City and County. So, I investigated our practices, thought about it, and wrote a page-and-a-half paper with recommendations for improving security. I suggested we lock the computers, lock the detective bureau at night, lock the gas pumps at night, and put reflective tape on the front windows so people couldn't do drive-by shootings, which happened in San Bernardino. I didn't want anyone to get hurt.

But our captain at the time was a loser and disregarded all my suggestions. We used to call him Captain Do Nothing. He was such a jerk. He didn't want to give the guys overtime because he

A photo I took during surveillance

wanted to cut down expenses to make it look good for promotion. His other nickname was Captain Kneepads. He wouldn't spend any money, even though it was pretty minimal, to improve station safety. He was willing to let his people get hurt rather than take measures to protect them. I wish it weren't that way, but with those who are political animals, it often is. My last statement in the report was, "It is like Pearl Harbor. Nothing gets done until something bad happens."

Anti-Shah Protest & the Wonders of Surveillance

In 1978, we were working surveillance during an anti-Shah protest in an undercover car on Wilshire Boulevard.

Things were a mess in Iran. The Shah, Mohammed Reza Pahlavi, was trying to modernize Iranian society, but people questioned his methods. For example, he imprisoned hundreds of clerics. He was also known to have a brutal secret police force, the SAVAK, funded by the U.S. There were all kinds of rumors about what the Shah was up to. I knew a guy who had become a TWA pilot after he left the military and did touch-and-go landings with Howard Hughes. He said that he flew pallets of gold from Iran to Switzerland for the Shah of Iran.

The voice of opposition to the modernization campaign was Ayatollah Khomeini, twice arrested and exiled. As major ideological tensions rose, anti-government demonstrations began in 1977, developing into a campaign of civil resistance. In August 1978, over 400 people died in a movie theater fire, claimed by the opposition as having been orchestrated by Pahlavi's SAVAK (After the war, an Islamic extremist admitted to it.) The incident came to serve as a catalyst for a revolutionary movement across all of Iran that paralyzed the entire country for the remainder of that year.

The revolution received a lot of support in the United States. In December 1978, the Iranian Student held a march up Market Street in San Francisco. The protests came to Los Angeles in 1979.

It was about one in the afternoon. People were marching with a poster that said, "Down with the Superpowers." People were shouting, "Fafasha! Fafasha! Death to the Shah!" To make me less conspicuous when doing the surveillance, I was wearing my "Jesus boots" and had loose long hair, no mustache or beard. Luckily, no violence erupted that day.

About thirty feet ahead of us was a Rolls Royce. All of a sudden, a female blonde head pops up in the passenger seat. "Hmm," I said to myself, "she must be looking for loose change on the floor." The man in the backseat with her was a famous athlete. I'm not sure if she was a prostitute or his date. That was unexpected at an anti-Shah rally. I certainly saw some things that were out of the ordinary when I worked surveillance.

You never knew what you'd see. Another time, I was one of a ten two-man crew doing surveillance on a bank robber in Hollywood. He always hit on Fridays. We knew what to look for if he got to the bank because he wore a certain kind of shoe and a Yankees baseball hat.

We were sitting half a block from the bank, waiting, and right next to us was a veterinary clinic. A yellow four-door Mercedes backed into the empty parking spot in front of us with personalized plates that read: MEOW. A lady got out and then pulled from her backseat a baby lion, probably three months old. I'd never seen anything like it.

We didn't catch a bank robber that day. He was eventually caught, but instead, that day, we witnessed a woman walking a baby lion into the vet clinic in the middle of Los Angeles.

Waiting for Homicide

Babysitting a homicide scene is no fun. This one was at an apartment house in Santa Monica, right on the beach. My partner that day, Charlie Martin, who was an ex-Navy Seal, and I had to secure the area around the apartment so it didn't get tainted before

Homicide showed up to do their thing and also while the crew was there to take away the corpse and gather evidence.

We were there for probably three hours. At one point, I had to go to the bathroom, so I went to this bar on the street level of the apartment building to use their john. It was 11:00 in the morning, and the place was filled with drunks already. Down a narrow hallway, I found the bathroom, but it was locked. The bartender said, "Oh, here's a key," which made me a little leery of the place. While I was using the bathroom, another guy came in. He walked over to me at the urinal and said, "If there's anything you need here, I can get it." I took my hand off my Johnson and put it on my gun. I thought, "If he starts fucking with me, I'm going to kill him." Thankfully, nothing happened. I laughed at myself after that, because in our job, you tended to be suspicious of any out-of-the-ordinary behavior.

Evicting a Felon-Squatter

Then came the case of the "squatter" in Westlake Village. I was working in Malibu as a detective when I got the case. A Mr. Dougherty called in and said, "I've got a $700,000 note on this house I own in Westlake Village. But I can't get the guy out of there, a Mr. Green, and he hasn't made a payment in six months."

Leon Green had moved into the mansion in the upscale area and filed for bankruptcy multiple times, so Doughtery couldn't do anything. But something was fishy about the situation. When I ran Leon's name, I discovered he was an ex-felon out of Atlanta and had a gun registered to him, which violated his parole. I also discovered that he obtained the lease to the house in a quick claim just before a triple homicide at the Encino Savings and Loan. An attorney, a banker, and woman were shot execution style. It was an LAPD homicide case, and they had no leads. I suspected Green was involved.

We went to the Westwood mansion with a SWAT team and

arrested Leon for illegal possession of a firearm. The house was trashed. There were pizza boxes everywhere, coat hangers—of all things—and soda cans all over the floor. The tub was stained green. Everything was disheveled.

I took the suspect in handcuffs out to the car. He had a Mercedes Benz 600 and asked, "Where be my car keys?"

"There be your car keys," I said and pointed at the tow truck. The car was in the process of getting repossessed. He hadn't made any payments on that either.

That was a good case. The owner of the house, which would probably be worth $8 million today, was thankful, however, there was no concrete evidence to link the suspect to the homicides. As far as I know, that case went unsolved.

The SLA and the Remiro-Little Case

In 1979, I was assigned to sit in as security on the high-profile case of People vs. Remiro. The Remiro-Little case involved two short pieces of human debris who were in the SLA, the Symbionese Liberation Army, the terrorist group famous for kidnapping Patty Hearst. The FBI and most law enforcement considered the SLA to be the first terrorist organization to rise from the American left.

In November of 1973, Remiro and Little had shot and killed Marcus Foster, a well-regarded and stand-up guy and the city of Oakland's first Black school superintendent. They also wounded the deputy superintendent, Robert Blackburn, targeting the two men as they left an Oakland school board meeting. Remiro and Little used hollow-point bullets that had been packed with cyanide. How sick is that? They were armed when they were arrested, which was dangerous for the arresting officers, but they were apprehended without an injury.

In 1974 six members of the SLA were later killed in a shootout with the LAPD. Remiro and Little were put in a local jail in San

Francisco. While incarcerated, they stabbed a deputy in the eye with a pencil. The deputy lost his eye because of these psychos.

It was because the case was so high profile that the judge sent it down to L.A., where I stood guard for the extent of the trial.

They couldn't identify the bullet that killed Mr. Foster because it had disintegrated so much. However, the gun they had used to commit the murder had an imperfection on the firing pin, a little snare. Luckily, the casing was found at the scene of the crime. It was discharged automatically when the automatic handgun was fired. In court, the prosecution presented a big photograph showing the back of the casing, and the forensic investigator showed where the imperfection in the firing pin in the .45 matched with the casing. So, they were both convicted.

While in prison, Russell Little claimed it was other members of the SLA who did the shooting of Foster and Blackburn. He also responded to the Patty Hearst kidnapping by saying he believed the SLA had entirely lost sight of its goals. His father, O. Jack Little, made a statement to the media and to other SLA members offering to take Patty Hearst's place as a kidnap victim. For better or worse, Little was acquitted in 1981 on a technicality, an error by the judge in instructing the jury. He now lives in Hawaii. But Remiro got life and is serving his time in Pelican Bay State Prison in Crescent City.

DEPUTY BOB MEAD
OFFICE OF THE UNDERSHERIFF
ORGANIZED CRIME BUREAU

211 W. TEMPLE STREET
LOS ANGELES, CA 90012   **SHERMAN BLOCK**
HALL OF JUSTICE   SHERIFF
(213) 974-4777   COUNTY OF LOS ANGELES

Boat Fraud

I was working with the detectives out of our headquarters when I was called on to investigate two individuals involved in a boat scam. One suspect was an insurance agent. The other worked with the Department of Motor Vehicles. The latter had obtained from his DMV office a bunch of blank boat permanent registration forms (CFs). Every boat, like every car, has to register and get a CF number. With that number, you can get your pink slip and insure a boat. The insurance company doesn't even need to see the boat. They trust the paperwork.

Seeing this weakness in the system, these two guys filled out all the registration forms with phony numbers for make-believe boats. They made them all Trojan brand, 35 feet long. A bunch of them "mysteriously sank" between Catalina, L.A., and San Pedro. They filed an insurance claim for $300,000 on each of the boats that never existed, yielding about two million dollars.

We got a hold of the boat builder in Florida. He said his company didn't make any boats that were longer than 29 feet. We told him we needed him to come out as a witness in the trial and assured him that we'd keep him safe. With his testimony, we were able to arrest the men and sentence them to prison in a grand jury indictment. Out on bail before their sentence started, one of the two men committed suicide, jumping off the Vincent Thomas Bridge.

Targeted by the Mob

The threat on my life started as an innocent conversation at my front door. My wife, Dona, was interested in religion. She was very intelligent and always questioned her beliefs. Some Mormon missionaries came by to talk to us about their faith. My wife listened to what they were saying. When I mentioned I was in law enforcement, this missionary had another story to tell me.

"Let me tell you about my sister and brother-in-law who have fallen away from the Mormon Church. They are into threesomes

238

```
                                                              CC: 707
AREA          29001 GARDEN OAKS CT., AGOURA
SUBJECT       DUNN, JEFFERY CRAIG (M/29)

DATE/TIME OCCURRENCE:  Current

SUMMARY:     Two local professional baseball players may be involved
             with illegal gambling and narcotics.

DETAILS:     Information from a confidential source is that one or
             more LOS ANGELES DODGERS may be involved in illegal
             gambling activities and cocaine useage.  This source
             states that STEVE HOWE and possibly STEVE SAX may
             have made bets and purchased cocaine from a JEFFERY C.
             DUNN (NIF), and that HOWE owes a large sum of money
             to DUNN.  JEFFERY DUNN lives in a $300,000 home and
             allegedly does his bookmaking and narcotics business
             from a private den at his residence.  Informant states
             that numerous times he has observed DUNN and STEVE HOWE
             enter this den area.  Also, DUNN has asked my source
             to handle weekend telephone bets, stating he would
             pay him $100.00 per day for five hours work.  DUNN
             gave the source in-depth instruction in how to handle
             the "betting line" on pro and college athletic events.
             The source declined involvement in this activity.
             The source further stated that he has never seen
             any cocaine at the DUNN location, but inferances
             were made by both DUNN and HOWE that narcotics are
             available there.

             My source feels HOWE is a heavy user of cocaine, and
             on one occasion, observed him to use cocaine prior
             to a Dodger game.  The other Dodger who has become
             quite friendly with JEFFERY DUNN is STEVE SAX.  SAX
             is rumored to be purchasing a home from DUNN.  DUNN,
             according to my informant, is not a realtor and
             doesn't work.  Recently, my source was told by DUNN
             that he would kill him if he said anything to
             authorities regarding his activities.
```

PRISONER'S SIG. FOR REC'T. OF REMAINING CASH & PROPERTY

One of several reports I filed on the Steve Howe/Jeffery Dunn case

and open marriages," he said, "It goes against our ways. But for my brother-in-law, there's more."

He told me the story of Mark Hopkinson and Jeff Green and the horrible crimes they were a part of. Mark Hopkinson was the first man executed in Wyoming since the 1960s for the murder of attorney Vincent Vehar, his wife Beverly, and their son John. Mark had ordered an associate to place a bomb in the basement of the Vehar home while the family was sleeping. At approximately 3:25 a.m., the bomb went off and destroyed the home, killing all three occupants. The murder plot arose from a water dispute in which Vincent Vehar represented the other party. Hopkinson was convicted of the murders yet always maintained his innocence. His last words were, "They have killed an innocent man."

While Hopkinson was in prison for the Vehars' murders, he contacted several people to find someone who would eliminate his former associate turned snitch, Jeff Green. Green had testified against Hopkinson during his trial as a federal witness. Hopkinson made statements that he would kill Green for what he had done.

Two days before he was set to testify to the grand jury against Hopkinson, Green's body was found in a state park on the Utah-Wyoming border. He had been tortured with a blowtorch, burned with cigarettes, beaten with a baseball bat, and fatally shot several times. The murder was deemed atrocious, heinous, and cruel.

The Mormon missionary informed me that he believed his brother-in-law was involved in Green's murder. He also said his brother-in-law had Mafia ties and was the cocaine dealer for Steve Howe, the famous baseball player.

I took that information to work, and it led us to conduct investigations on the brother-in-law, Jeffery Dunn. We pulled trash out of his bins to get information on our suspect, transporting it with a trash truck at four in the morning to an open field where we sifted through it. The suspect claimed he didn't make much money, but we found bank statements and expensive bottles of wine, and he lived in a very expensive house. We got the IRS involved since it was clear that he was hiding money.

We eventually had enough evidence to arrest him on tax evasion and, with a search warrant, we found a large quantity of cocaine and $10,000 at his residence, so we got him on possession and dealing too.

After that went down, the baseball player Steve Howe visited us at the station. He was scared. He said he might be the target of a hit by the Mafia. He also claimed that I might get hit because I was active in the investigation. This was no small threat. The ties to the Mafia were real.

I went to my chief, Ollie Taylor. He was a good friend. I said, "Ollie, send me to Hawaii for two weeks."

"No. It won't happen. Do you want security?"

"No. I've got enough guns."

My wife knew how to shoot. My son knew how to shoot. But we were all on alert for months, and I filed multiple reports.

COUNTY OF LOS ANGELES	SHERIFF'S DEPARTMENT

MEMORANDUM Date 6-28-84

File No.

From: Dep R. Mead   061157   To: A/LT. Stiver

Subject: Threat to a Deputy

    I received information from two seperate reliable informants; both stated they had conversations with Dodger Relief Pitcher Steve Howe on 6-27, 6-28-84. Howe told them to tell me and also an unk. DEA (?) Agent to "Watch our backs." He also stated that he found a note in his mail box approximately one week ago stating, "Tell Bob Mead to watch his back." (I have never talked with Steve Howe). He further related that I should be concerned with a Detroit hit-man, drug runner possibly named "Chinner" (unk. spelling or a nick-name). This man apparently drives a white Jaguar and travels extensively between L.A. and Arizona transporting drugs.
    It should be noted that writer did an extensive investigation on Steve Howe and Jeffery Dunn. Dunn was a suspect in a quadruple Wyoming murder case that is still under investigation. (See reports). Because of my investigation of Dunn, I.R.S. Agent Tom Schenk has started a complete tax audit on his activities, which coincidentally began approximately one week ago.

R. W. Mead #061157

☐ FOR YOUR INFORMATION.   ☐ REPORT ON RESULTS REQUIRED.   ☐ VERBAL REPORT ONLY, CONFIDENTIAL

COHEN, David Sam

Last name	First	Middle

AKA: Possible/CHINNER, David

D.O.B. 09-29-37
P.O.B.
Age _____ Race M/W
Ht. 5'8" Wt. 250
Hair Bro Eyes Grn
Dr. lic. No. N2377943   Photo
Soc. Sec.
FBI 26 1490
CII
No. 1
No. 2

Addresses
Present: 4680 Limerick Ln., Las Vegas
Previous: 1431 Maple Hills Rd., Diamond Bar

Vehicles
Yr. It Make Jag Mod. XKE Color wht
Lic. No. NV 664 AMN
Yr. Make Mod. Color

Previous mugshot of the identified hit man, David "Chinner" Cohen, who was supposed to take me out. He was working for Anthony "Tony the Ant" Spilotro who served as the basis for the character Nicky Santoro in Martin Scorsese's 1995 film Casino.

The guy went to prison, and things settled down. But we spent the next year looking in our mailboxes and under our cars to ensure there were no bombs. Ultimately, it was all okay.

During this time, my wife and I joined the Mormon Church. We got remarried in the temple. We even wore the traditional white temple undergarments. We did baptisms for the dead. We took a group of kids to the Junior Olympics in Colorado. It was fun and interesting. I was brought up Catholic, although my family didn't practice much.

Dona and I ended up giving up Mormonism to practice independent faith, I guess you would call it. We prayed. I still do. I go to church with friends occasionally. I practice the Golden Rule and charity to others.

One more comment about religion before I leave it alone. Religion helps a lot of people, but I think religious leaders are wrong when they demonize people for having "alternative" lifestyles. I've worked with a lot of people: colleagues, folks on the streets, and prisoners in jail. At the end of the day, I believe in treating everyone with respect and judging people by their character and not their sexuality, gender, color, or culture. As I've said before, my greatest joy is helping others. To this day, if I see someone in need, I want to help them, whether it's with a few bucks or a conversation to make them feel seen and heard.

Rock Thrower on the Freeway

I had been visiting one of my partners who was in the hospital. A heavy smoker, he had suffered a heart attack. Driving home in my own car in plain clothes, I took the transition road from the Pomona Freeway to the Ventura Freeway. I had just entered the on-ramp when a large rock hit my windshield hard, the glass breaking and spiderwebbing out. I immediately pulled to the curb, jumped out of my car, and pulled my gun, looking for the suspect, angry as hell. There's no way a rock that size could get kicked up from the road.

242

Someone had thrown it, and if it had gone through the window, it would have killed me. At that moment, I felt like I could have shot that cockroach if I had seen him, although I'm sure my training would've kicked in. Had I caught the guy, I would've chewed him out plenty, but I would've followed procedure. That's what you do.

Not seeing anyone, I went home. The next day, I sent a teletype to the LAPD about the incident. They caught the culprit that day, a Mexican-American kid just under 18. He had also thrown a muffler from an overpass through the window of an 18-wheeler. That's very dangerous. An 18-wheeler out of control can do a lot of damage on a freeway. Luckily, the truck driver responded calmly and was able to pull off the road. He wasn't injured but did have to shave his head because of all the glass shards in his hair.

The kid was sent to the California Youth Authority. I don't know if he had a motive, was just being stupid, or was mentally challenged. But it shows you that even an off-duty cop can be the victim of random crime. And it helped that I had an inside line of communication.

A.M. in Arson & Explosives

I dealt with tough situations sometimes, but the guys in Arson & Explosives Division had the most dangerous job on the force; they had to deal with live bombs. One of the guys, Arlee McRee, or A.M., was one of the top bomb squad technicians in the country. He had defused or safely removed many bombs from public places and saved a lot of lives. But his luck ran out. A special effects man in the movie industry had built a bomb in his Studio City house. The man blew up cars and faux buildings on movie sets for a living, so he knew how to make a bomb. Somehow, the LAPD found out and brought in the bomb squad, with A.M. as the leader. He was trying to defuse the bomb when it exploded. He was killed on the job. The man who made the bomb was arrested for murder. The story was reported widely in that evening's news. That was a sad one.

CHAPTER 18

FIST "Delivery Service"

I WORKED WITH THE U.S. MARSHAL SERVICE once again in 1984 as part of their Fugitive Investigative Strike Teams, also known as FIST operations. The goal of FIST was to locate and arrest large numbers of mostly violent-crime fugitives in particular areas within a relatively brief time period by focusing the resources of local, state, and Federal law enforcement agencies. I was one of 120 guys on the team selected for advanced training as Enforcement Specialists dedicated to overseeing the investigation and apprehension of Federal fugitives nationwide. I was working Los Angeles County, but as a U.S. Marshal deputy, I could cross city, county, and state boundaries with full arrest powers.

Part of our strategy was to set up this great, simple and effective "scam," similar to what we had been doing in the Detective Department, but even better. We sent notices to fugitives' last known addresses asking them to arrange for acceptance of a package worth up to $2,000. They just needed to arrange delivery with the "FIST Bonded Delivery Courier Service." These guys would get curious and greedy, dial the number on the notification, which happened to be a Marine barracks in Pico Rivera, and a "service representative," AKA U.S. Marshal would pick up the phone and confirm an address where we could meet them for delivery.

Then came the sting: A Ford van with a FIST Bonded Delivery Courier Service sign on the side arrived at the target's address. A maroon-shirted driver went to the door and asked if the recipient could step outside to sign a receipt for the package. The moment the fugitive signed, confirming his identity, two teams of officers—of which I was a part—sprang out of our cars to make the arrest.

The fugitives were very surprised to get handcuffs instead of their packages! Sometimes they just didn't get what was going on. One guy said, "Hey, that guy had a package for me!" Another one said, "You don't have to be so mean! That truck was delivering me a package."

Sixty-five appointments were made by wanted fugitives for these "packages." Other methods were used to make more arrests.

There were several phases of FIST around the nation. Ours in California, FIST VI, was by far the most successful. The ten-week operation resulted in 2,116 arrests. Of those arrested 79 percent had been involved in crimes of violence or drug offenses and a total of 2,689 cases were closed as a result of the arrests.

The operation was also highly cost-efficient by utilizing existing resources of more than 20 California state and local law enforcement agencies, like me, which made up half of the 120-member FIST VI group. Like the previous U.S. Marshal work I did, they provided the money, we provided the local expertise and were already trained to do the job well. There was strong camaraderie and a high degree of professional motivation exhibited by our combined team. The Feds paid $1.7 million for the program, which came out to around $800 per fugitive captured. And most of that expense was to complete the arrest in Sonoma County of accused Drug Trafficker Rexford Andrew Ramsey. We confiscated his ranch, valued at $1.5 million, two properties in Miami, three Formula One race cars, and $500,000 in cash. When Ramsey was convicted, the Marshals auctioned off the proceeds to zero out the cost of the Fist Operation. Now that's Federal money well-managed!

The operation got extensive media coverage in all of the major television networks, weekly news magazines, and principal newspapers throughout the nation. Former U.S. Marshal Director Stanley E. Morris described FIST as "possibly the largest and most successful fugitive hunt in recent history." It was beautiful! It felt good to be a part of it.

Nation

FIST by a K.O.

The feds reel in the fugitives

It was a gorgeous scam, simple in design, swift in execution. It worked like a dream, 65 times in ten weeks. The setup: a fugitive from justice in the Los Angeles area receives notice at his last known address that a package containing $2,000 worth of unspecified goods is waiting for him at FIST Bonded Delivery Courier Service. Curiosity piqued and greed aroused, he calls the number on the notice to arrange delivery. The number he dials happens to be a Marine barracks in Pico Rivera in Los Angeles County. The person he speaks with is working for the U.S. Marshals Service.

being sought for violent crimes, and on the average each had five felony counts on his record. The criminals included 24 accused or convicted murderers, 39 rapists, 13 kidnapers and 272 robbers. Said Marshals Director Stanley Morris of FIST: "I cannot think of any more successful operation in such a time span."

According to Morris, 210,000 fugitive felony warrants are outstanding in the U.S. While crime rates in general may have dropped slightly, the number of fugitives has increased 17% in the past two years. Financial constraints, jurisdictional restrictions and limited manpower can prevent local law officers from actively pursuing fugitives. Police must concentrate on fresh crimes, the bank robbery or murder that has just been committed.

The California man hunt was a spe-

Marshal Larry Carter, in FIST disguise, with the van that helped trick fugitives

As agents handcuffed him, one felon screamed, "Hey, that guy had a package for me!"

FIST, featured in Time Magazine, *March 1984*

U.S. DEPARTMENT OF JUSTICE
UNITED STATES MARSHALS SERVICE

OATH OF OFFICE - SPECIAL DEPUTATION
(See reverse side for instructions)
(Ref. Order USM 1036.1)

EXPIRATION DATE
OF SPECIAL
DEPUTATION

March 20,1984

CENTRAL District of CALIFORNIA

I, ROBERT MEAD , do solemnly swear (or affirm) that I will faithfully execute all lawful precepts directed to the United States Marshal for the Central District of California or to the appropriate Federal official as so designated, under the authority of the United States, make true returns, take only lawful fees, and in all things well and truly, without malice or partiality, perform the duties of the Office of Special Deputy United States Marshal during my continuance in that office. I will exercise my authorities under this Special Deputation solely in furtherance of the mission for which I have been specially deputized and only during my continuance under this Special Deputation. So help me God.

(SIGNATURE OF APPOINTEE)

Subscribed and Sworn to be before me this 5th day of January , 19 84 ,
at Los Angeles , California
(City) (State)

Julio Gonzales
(SIGNATURE OF OFFICER)

U.S. Marshal
(TITLE)

*RESTRICTIONS: Valid only while performing official duties during F.I.S.T. VI Operation

NOT VALID UNLESS CERTIFIED BELOW BY DIRECTOR OR DEPUTY DIRECTOR OF THE UNITED STATES MARSHALS SERVICE, OR BY A UNITED STATES MARSHAL:

I certify that the above-named individual, having taken the Oath of Office, is authorized to perform the duties of the Office of Special Deputy United States Marshal under this deputation on the 5th day of January , 1984 .

Julio Gonzales
AUTHORIZED CERTIFYING OFFICIAL

Appointee's Employer: Los Angeles Sheriffs Office
Sponsoring Federal Agency: U.S. Marshals Service
Appointee's Supervisor during Special Deputation: Julio Gonzales
(Name of appropriate United States Marshal or designated Federal official)

Physical Description: Height 6'1" Weight 175 Sex M Race W Color Eyes Blu Hair Brn

SUPERSEDES FORM USM-218
WHICH MAY 'SED

Form USM-3
(Est 3/6/80)

Officially deputized—again—by the U.S. Marshal service for Operation FIST

The Truth Will Set You Free

County of Los Angeles
Office of the Sheriff
Hall of Justice
Los Angeles, California 90012

SHERMAN BLOCK, SHERIFF

April 18, 1984

Robert Grant Mead
2199 Calaveras Drive
Camarillo, California 93010

Dear Deputy Mead:

I wish to take this opportunity to personally commend you on your
recent efforts on the Fugitive Investigative Strike Team. Although
you and the other members of the Los Angeles County Sheriff's
Department represented only 30% of the F.I.S.T. Teams in the Los
Angeles area, your 352 combined arrests totalled 41% of the arrests
made in the area.

You and your partner, Deputy U.S. Marshal Tomas Lopez, were personally
responsible for 41 arrests while working over 200 hours of overtime
in the short ten week period the Task Force functioned. Your
professional demeanor and expertise in making these arrests while
working with a partner from Phoenix, Arizona who was unfamiliar
with this area, has resulted in this being the most successful
Fugitive Task Force in United States history.

The removal of these violent offenders and career criminals from
the streets of our community constitutes a great public service,
and the Department is extremely proud of your record during this
operation.

Sincerely,

SHERMAN BLOCK, SHERIFF

ROBERT A. EDMONDS
ASSISTANT SHERIFF

Commendation for Operation FIST

CHAPTER 19

Wayside Honor Ranch, 1985–1988

I HAD BEEN PATROLLING ALL OVER L.A. COUNTY for nearly 26 years. It was time to get off the streets. I ended my career where I began, working in a jail, this time at Wayside Honor Ranch on the outskirts of L.A. County near Magic Mountain amusement park. I was still living in Camarillo, and Wayside was the closest to home, making for an easy commute.

One of the farms at Wayside Honor Ranch around 1960, teaching real skills to inmates

Wayside Honor Ranch wasn't like a regular jail. The Sheriff's Department ran it as a working farm that produced milk and meat on 3,000 acres. The inmates slept in open barracks, but there were cells for disciplinary holding. They had a lot of training and educational programs to help the men reenter society when they got out.

There were three facilities at the ranch. One of the facilities was minimum security for first-time sentence prisoners. Then there was a medium-security facility. These were people waiting to go to court on $10,000 bail or less. There was also a maximum-security facility for prisoners with high bail.

Wayside Honor Ranch

I worked as a supervisor, running the laundry. I oversaw both inmates and deputies. We processed about two million pounds of laundry a month from all the jails, including from Juvenile Hall, the female jails, and hospitals. The laundry ran sixteen hours a day, and I had five inmates and ten deputies working for me. I set down my expectations, treated them with respect, and never had a problem with any of them.

Los Angeles Times

LAUNDRY: It All Comes Out in Wash —Tons of It

Continued from Page 1

T-shirts, underwear, sheets, pillow cases, gowns and jumpsuits every week.

About 55% of the dirty laundry handled by Budds' crew is generated by the county's 21,000 jail inmates. The balance comes from five county hospitals—High Desert Hospital in Lancaster, Olive View Medical Center in Sylmar and the pediatric, psychiatric and women's hospitals at County-USC Medical Center—which send their patient gowns, doctors smocks, bed sheets and surgery linens here. Next year, the County-USC General Hospital

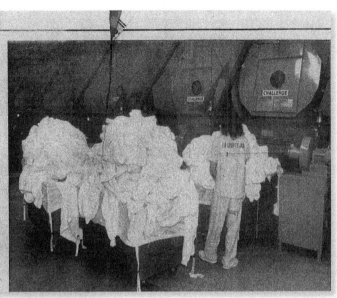

Inmate helpers are dwarfed by mountain of laundry, a daily challenge at Pitchess Honor Rancho. STEVE DYKES / Los Angeles Times

WHITE WASH

County Honor Farm Laundry Cleans Up on 25 Tons of Clothes Daily—a Big Pile on Anyone's Back Porch

By TOM GORMAN, *Times Staff Writer*

Meet Harry Budds, rhymes with suds, lord of laundry. You're cursing a load of sheets and a pile of whites and Budds is staring at 50,000 pounds of clothes and sheets and towels—every day. That's 4,000 loads to you and me.

Talk about shoveling sand against the Tide.

Budds may well run the largest institutional laundry service in the country, with the help of 57 paid workers and 500 men who don't get a cent. If that sounds criminal, it's because they are.

Budds is administrator of laundry services at the sprawling Pitchess Honor Rancho near Saugus, home to 7,000 inmates, under the care and feeding of the Los Angeles County Sheriff's Department. They're all men—half of them awaiting sentencing and the other half serving time for misdemeanors and less-serious felonies—and while they bide their time here, they're assigned various jobs, ranging from the rancho's dairy to furniture repair.

Some men are sent to the laundry, where they sort, wash, dry, fold and stack 250,000 pairs of socks.

Please see LAUNDRY, Page 9

STEVE DYKES / Los Angeles Times

Manager Xavier de La Piedra, left, and top boss Harry Budds up to hips in clean laundry.

I supervised the processing of a lot of laundry!

I also took time away from the laundry to train new deputies prior to them going out on patrol, the same way I was trained 25 years ago. I even trained some officers from London who worked for Her Majesty's Prison Service. It sounds very royal, but they had hardened criminals and gangs in London, just like we did, except they didn't have the same firepower to deal with them.

These English guys had never fired a gun. They had never handled handguns, shotguns, A.R.s, or anything. They loved everything we showed them and learned fast out on the range. When we showed them how to shoot teargas, they just about went crazy.

It was fun being at the jail. I had good partners and a good team. The brass liked me because I was dependable and I took care of problems. I helped other officers deal with the escape problem at Wayside.

A gift from the British police

There used to be a lot of escapes because it was so open and didn't have the security of a normal prison. Guys could just walk off the property if they wanted to. I gave presentations to fellow deputies about how to deal with escapes. My program cut the escapes down to almost zero.

One of the strategies was to talk matter-of-factly to the inmates about the consequences of escape. I used to tell them, "Look, if you've got a problem, come see me. Because here's what's going to happen if you escape. You'll get caught. You'll get a bullet in jail." A bullet means an extra year locked up. "And you won't be sent back to a facility like this one. It will be maximum security behind bars." I said, "You'd be stupid to try it."

You get to know the inmates. These are real people, most of whom did something stupid, got involved with drugs or the wrong crowd, or lacked real values or boundaries because they were young, ignorant, damaged, and sometimes just lacking brain cells. I got a real laugh when an inmate came in with the same name as me, Bob Mead. He was a young Black guy, a decent kid, and really scared.

I asked him, "Bob Mead? How are Mom and Dad?" Everyone laughed. It broke the ice.

We dealt with a lot of mental illness in the jail. That was challenging. When an inmate acted stupid, he earned himself some disciplinary time. As a supervisor, I had the authority to reward inmates or take good behavior time away from people or make their sentences longer for misbehaving. This one inmate got access to a civilian's car and slept in the back seat. When I asked him about it, he gave me some song and dance, telling me he was Satan. That day, there were six other inmates standing in line for disciplinary time along with him. The guy who said he was Satan was white. The others, facing discipline for tattooing or minor theft, were Black and Mexican, so I knew they didn't run in the same groups. The jails are pretty segregated places. The inmates create the distinctions themselves. I said, "Okay, guys, we're going to play Caesar in the Coliseum."

I explained about the gladiators. They were into the history lesson. "Okay, so if you believe Satan here, thumbs up. If you don't, thumbs down." They all gave a thumbs down. I told them, "Get out of here, guys. I don't want to give you any disciplinary time. I've got to deal with Satan." I put Satan on the disciplinary crew, breaking rocks.

I had a good relationship with the inmates, and word got around. I never showed them disrespect. If they had an attitude, I responded to the attitude. The guy who wanted to be called Satan found that out. Most inmates appreciated being treated fairly and with respect. And, just like in the beginning of my career, they used to help me out. We had vending machines with Coke and other soft drinks, cookies, candy, and stuff like that. An ARA employee (Automatic Retailers of America, Inc., the vending company) was at the jail filling the machines and stopped to eat lunch. People who worked at the jail, even the vendors, could eat free at the jail. But the guy forgot to lock his truck. He had $1,600 in there, collected from other vending machines. In the meantime, someone went into his truck and took the money. Shaken, he reported the missing money to me as soon as he discovered it was gone. Shortly after, an inmate approached me and said, "You're straight with the inmates. So, I'll be straight with you. The money is in one of the barracks." He told me where to find it. We sent deputies in there and recovered $1,300 of the $1,600. Honesty tops everything. When your honest there's no other way to go. If your honest, you don't mistreat people. There's no need for excuses. There's no need for shame, for guilt, for hiding. In contrast, when you lie, you're stepping in horse manure and stuck cleaning up after yourself.

They closed the farming operations in the early 1990s due to budget cuts. And it's now the Peter J. Pitchess Detention Center. It's a shame. The farming was good for the guys. And though the open facility required more thoughtful supervision, I think that was good for the inmates too. It made those who could handle it more responsible. Luckily, the farm has been replaced with other "realignment" programs. The North County Correctional Facility was built in 1990 and offers vocational training in printing, baking, and clothes manufacturing. The South Facility's Fire Camp Training Facility allows inmates convicted of non-serious, nonviolent, and nonsexual offenses to train as firefighters. Those guys have helped out a lot with all the California wildfires. For a long time, it was the county's largest jail complex and is still the oldest operating jail in the county.

For a few years afterwards, I received thank you letters from previous inmates. I've included two of them. Cunningham was a forgerer who made phony credit cards with numbers he procured from a bank teller. He provided her with cocaine in exchange. He went and blew all the money in Las Vegas on gambling and prostitutes. The other, Tony, was a karate instructor who had an affair with an unerage karate student. Both went straight after prison. After they were released and were rebuilding their lives, they took with them the kindness, respect and straightforwardness I showed them while they were incarcerated. It meant something to them. And that means a lot to me.

COUNTY OF LOS ANGELES   **SHERIFF'S DEPARTMENT**

MEMORANDUM   Date _____

File No. _____

From: _Cunningham_   To: _Sr. Mead_

Subject: _____

YES I AM OUT OF COUNT FOR GOOD I JUST WANT TO let YOU
KNOW THAT FOR THE TIME I SPENT WITH YOU I FOUND OUT THAT
YOU ARE ONE OF THE FEW GOOD MEN I HAVE HAD THE PLEASURE
OF DOING TIME WITH I HOPE FOR YOU AND YOUR FAMILY THE BEST
OF HEALTH AND HAPPINESS FOR ALL THE DAYS TO COME.

CUNNINGHAM

P.S.
HOW ABOUT SOME
COOKIES

☐ FOR YOUR INFORMATION.

Letters of appreciation from previously incarcerated guys. The key for me was having boundaries and exercising kindness. Kindness comes back to you. At least that's been my experience.

12/18/85

Bob,
I hope you and your family enjoy the vacation and the holidays.
You do a lot of good for a lot of people not only in the material sense but what I consider more important, as an "example" which is desperately needed by the types of people who pass through the "system".
To stand by your beliefs and principles is only something a strong person can do on a consistent basis. Over the months I've known you I've seen you demonstrate this consistency, many, many times. I have a deep respect for you for being this way and for the man you are. Because your type of man is seldom understood, let alone appreciated I just want to put in writing my appreciation and recognition of your inner qualities, which are the true indicators of a man. Your actions speak for you and they are of the highest quality.
I hope happiness and good health follows you, your family and loved ones wherever you go.
Merry Christmas!
Happy New Year!
Happy Life!

OS!

Tony

CHAPTER 20

Teaching Security in Samoa

T REATING OTHERS WITH RESPECT has been one of the greatest things I've learned in all my years in law enforcement. More times than I can count, it has paid dividends. This is true in my personal life as well. I think it's what first made me attractive to the most amazing woman I've ever known.

Loving Dona

Dona and I had forty-five glorious years together before she passed away. The only difference between us was our plumbing. We were that much alike. We never fought. Being married to Dona showed me even more clearly that my first two marriages had been mistakes and why that was the case. I married my first wife because she got pregnant, and I wanted to do the right thing. We were so young. Though I cared about her and about my second wife, we hadn't loved each other in a deep, unconditional way. I'm not sure I even understood the concept or knew it was possible, so it took a lot of mistakes to find the woman of my dreams and true, shared love. I told Dona, "In you, I have met my match."

She was there for me. She was always there for me. I worked twelve-hour days for the U.S. Marshals, driving sixty-seven miles from Pico Rivera to the Marine Reserve in Camarillo. She never complained once. She was the best at everything, and she opened up my world.

I had never traveled outside the country before I met Dona; I had only traveled to a few places domestically. Dona worked as a flight attendant because she loved to travel and knew how. We enjoyed quite a few adventures across the globe. We went to World War II sites, places of historical significance that she knew I would like. We visited the Guernsey Islands, Normandy, Bastogne, and the Ardennes Forest. Our itinerary stretched from Budapest to Amsterdam—an incredible experience! On a river cruise in Vienna, Austria, we danced a Strauss Waltz, which was unforgettable. We also went to places she was interested in: the Greek Islands, Istanbul, and Athens. It was just spectacular. In 1974, Dona and I took a trip to the South Pacific. We went to Tahiti and the Marquesas Islands for fourteen days, an unforgettable experience. One of our stops along the way was Hiva Oa, where we visited the grave of the French artist Paul Gauguin.

With Dona in the South Pacific

Paul had lived in Tahiti for several years before succumbing to syphilis and dying in 1903. His grave was marked with a simple cross and had become something of a tourist attraction.

257

We stopped in Bora Bora, where we took a tour of the island's many lagoons and reefs. We also visited Moorea, off the coast of Tahiti. We saw where they filmed the movie, *South Pacific*. It was breathtakingly beautiful!

We traveled to Namibia and Mozambique. Nine months before Dona died, we took a trip around South Africa. She made my life a bigger place, full of adventure. I still grieve for her. Not a day goes by that I don't miss her.

New Addition

My two children were living with their mother when Dona and I married, and as soon as I could, I introduced them to my new wife. The kids seemed drawn to Dona right away. She was very understanding and giving, so I think they felt comfortable with her and respected her. I was so pleased. We took them on a trip to Puerto Vallarta and did regular house boating trips on Shasta Lake in Northern California.

Dona had never been a mother and longed to be, so we decided to have a child together. In 1975, our son was born. I was 49 years old. With Dona at the helm, everything went as smoothly as possible, given the ins and outs of parenthood. We hadn't planned to travel again with a baby to care for, but that same year, I was offered an opportunity that neither of us wanted to refuse.

American Samoa

One day, my partner at the Lennox Station, Bill Hallick, approached me with an intriguing proposition. He asked, "Hey, do you want to teach a class on security in American Samoa?"

I said, "Sure!" Dona and I were excited about the opportunity to visit the island country and I felt good about the assignment. Although I didn't possess a college degree, I earned a teaching credential from the State of California in 1972-73. The county had offered it for free to build their pool of qualified teachers and substitute teachers, in light of a serious shortage. I took 40 hours of courses, mostly at night, on teaching practices, techniques, and strategies and on knowing your students. I didn't plan to move into teaching any time soon, but it seemed like a great opportunity to jump on in case I wanted to teach in a community college when I retired. I figured the certificate might open up more doors in life. And, at the least, would further my understanding of people. Armed with training films from the Sheriff's Department, I knew I had something to teach about security and could do it effectively.

We left our nearly one-year-old securely in the hands of my mother-in-law and father-in-law and embarked on the two-week teaching assignment, first flying from LAX to Hawaii on a Pan Am 707. There, we were greeted by friends of Bill Hallick living on Oahu. They graciously took us to dinner, and then we flew on to Samoa. Originally from Hawaii, Bill and his wife Twinkle greeted us and hosted us in their family home in Pago Pago. I brought them steaks, frozen in dry ice, and a case of Coors beer, things they couldn't get on the island.

In Samoa

From the get-go, the locals we met were incredibly warm, friendly, and welcoming. The Polynesian culture in American Samoa centers around faith, family, community, and music, as it has since prehistoric times. They look after each other, which helps since there's not a lot of money around. They regularly face severe tropical storms, and they survived a history of foreign takeovers. After many European missionaries came and went in the 18th century, the United States took possession of the island in the late 19th century and made it into a central naval outpost in the Pacific that was a strategic boon in the South Pacific theater of World War II. In 1967, the territory became self-governing with the adoption of a constitution. To this day, the people of

Enjoying our exploration and meeting people

Samoa have no voting representation in the U.S. Congress, and even though they're in American-controlled territory, they are not granted U.S. citizenship at birth.

But for us two-week visitors, it felt like paradise, complete with perfect beaches and an open market on the weekends where we could buy everything from bananas and tropical fruit to seafood and hand-crafted clothes. The hot, humid weather didn't bother us a bit.

Such hospitality!

Getting ready to teach in Samoa

Bill's father, the Samoan chief, took me to all the other chiefs in the area. They offered me a drink called kava. This peculiar white substance resembled dish soap and was rumored to have narcotic properties, but it didn't affect me.

The class I taught for those two weeks covered airport, industrial, and presidential security and was well-received. I had brought along films and shared a lot of our "war stories" fighting crime in the Los Angeles County Sheriff's office. By contrast, there was a Highway Patrol lieutenant presenting a class on law enforcement, but his curriculum didn't make any sense. To show you how incompetent the government can sometimes be, this

261

fellow, though a decent guy, was there giving a class on radar use for traffic control that was paid for with federal money. American Samoa had very few cars. People mostly got around riding bicycles, motorcycles, horses, donkeys, and wagons. Only one main road

went halfway around the island and contained very little traffic. On top of this, the poor traffic cop was fairly new to the force and didn't know much of anything, having little experience in the field. I guess he taught in his uniform to create some sense of authority, but he was timid and sweaty, like Linda Lovelace going to church.

Over our final weekend, Dona and I flew to the island of Western Samoa in British territory, about 50 miles away. Dona went off to explore on her own while I went fishing on a brand-new boat owned by a local

fisherman. As we went to the fishing spot, we encountered a group of Samoans fishing in outrigger canoes several miles from land. Their dedication to the craft, with no modern luxuries like GPS or even bathrooms, left a lasting impression on me. Unfortunately, the boat's rocking motion made me seasick, resulting in me christening the vessel. The captain dropped me back off at the dock and then went out and caught the biggest marlin he'd ever caught in his life. He cooked it for us for dinner that night at his restaurant. I was feeling better by then and was able to eat the fish, thankfully.

The Samoan people were exceptionally nice to us. Their meat consisted of fish and bats, which they shot out of the coconut palms. We learned that every two weeks, a steamship from New Zealand brought supplies, food, beer and other drinks, catsup, and all kinds of things that couldn't be grown or manufactured on an island with its limited resources. As a result, the only beer available was New Zealand Leopard beer, and we drank a lot of that.

The next day, Dona and I toured the island by Jeep on bumpy dirt roads. We saw turkeys and pigs running around along with naked kids about three or four years old. Being unused to that, I found the sight funnier than hell. Beneath a seminary, we found this stunning freshwater lagoon in a natural grotto and went swimming in crystal-clear water surrounded by breathtaking beauty. Another vivid memory, captured in a photograph, is Dona and me in front of Robert Louis Stevenson's old white-washed house in Western Samoa. The writer, nomadic by nature, didn't mean to but ended up settling there since the climate was good for his delicate health. He wrote a lot about the Polynesian islands and people.

I got the chills while flying back on our DC-3 from Western Samoa to American Samoa. It was very hot and humid, so it made no sense. Then I started sweating like crazy. I went to Lyndon Johnson Socialized Medicine Hospital, where they told me I had contracted dengue fever. A doctor gave me some medicine and a shot. In about two weeks, I got over it. Socialized medicine meant it didn't cost me any money at all.

The people of Western Samoa left an indelible mark on my heart. Although I only learned two Samoan words, *talofa* and *fa'afetai*, which mean hello and thank you, they didn't hold it against me! That's a trip I'll never forget.

The Space Shuttle Enterprise

Being a deputy wasn't a high-paying job, but as I said, there were perks. I made some great friends and contacts, and they often provided me with unique opportunities. One of my partners whom I'd known for years, Gene Bernhard, had retired from Dope—what we called the Narcotics unit—and was working plainclothes security at the NASA Rockwell facility in Palmdale, where they were building the very first Space Shuttle, *Enterprise*. He called me and said, "Come on up. I'll show you around." Perhaps it helped that I had clearance as a deputy.

Dona and I toured the place, learning about the entire construction process. I got photographs, including one of the gold leafs they put inside. I even got to bring home a piece of the tiles they used on the shuttle. Towards the end of construction, we watched them pre-heat these very light silica tiles, white as paper and light as a feather, in a contraption that looked like a big pizza oven on rollers. The tiles came out red hot. I asked one of the technicians, "How soon can you touch it?" Twenty seconds later, he could pick it up. I could picture them heating up on reentry into the atmosphere but having the ability to cool down very quickly. It was unbelievable.

No Longer Checking Out the Talent

I went from a rookie who manned the jail to a detective who saw patterns and criminals everywhere. I lost a lot of good friends along the way. I saw some good cops die. On and off the job, I was always very aware of my surroundings wherever I went and always had a gun. My instincts were sharp, which was good for work but bad for a marriage. It made for tense conversations with Dona whenever we went out to eat. Rather than talk to her, I spent my time on the lookout for criminals or suspicious activities. And sometimes, Dona mistook that for me checking out the women. I never cheated on Dona. I was clean as a whistle with her. But still, she would watch me suspiciously and ask, "Are you checking out the women, Rob?"

I'd reply, "No, I am not checking out the talent. I'm looking to see if the bad guys are a problem." Then, to prove it to her, I'd point to a guy and say, "That guy's dirty." Or point to another and say, "I don't trust that guy." She would look at them, nod, and go back to eating. Being a cop's wife was hard, but Dona handled it well. She was so understanding. And, once retired, I worked to beat the habit.

Out of L.A.

After I retired, we wanted to leave California to move somewhere quieter. There were so many people in Los Angeles County, so much traffic. If I wanted to go anywhere, it could take two hours just to cross over the county line. But mainly, I was tired

Dona and I visiting the old SWAT headquarters. She listened patiently to lots of old stories!

of scanning my surroundings, looking for suspicious characters. It became too nerve-wracking to live in a populous place. Also, I wanted to get my youngest son out of Los Angeles before he started high school and finish bringing him up where kids could be kids.

We moved to Bend, Oregon, and bought a beautiful two-and-a-half-acre piece of property surrounded by a national forest. Dona designed her dream house and we built it. It was a gorgeous house. At the time, Bend had little traffic and no gangs. My son attended Bend High School and joined the Mount Bachelor ski team. He keeps thanking me for getting him out of California because some of his friends that stayed have fallen by the wayside from drugs and things like that. Where I live now, I walk across the street daily to a national forest and the sparkling Deschutes River.

Losing Dona

Like me, Dona was never a drinker. Her grandfather, a colonel in World War I, was an alcoholic, and her father, a B-17 pilot in World War II, was an alcoholic. Dona didn't want to go that route. The evening after seeing the space shuttle at Rockwell, we went to a Mexican restaurant in Palmdale, Dona splurged and had two margaritas, which was a rare occurrence.

"Do you guys remember that dope case you had?" she asked me and my buddy.

I said, "Which one?"

"The big one," she said, "You're going to go down in the anals of history."

I smiled. "No, Dona, you mean the annals of history."

"Nope," she grinned, "the anals of history."

We laughed hard that night.

Dona was still a head-turner at seventy-three, with great pins and a great smile. I'll tell you that.

She always said to me, "You're the best thing on two legs."

I'd joke in response, "I'm so good I could run for Pope."

It was devastating when she was diagnosed with ovarian cancer in 2016. She gave me a Rolex just before she died that I wear now most of the time. She was put in hospice when she got really ill.

The ladies took good care of her, but it was hard. Dona was in so much pain. "Give me a gun. Just give me a gun," she said to me. Still, they managed to ease her suffering some. I rarely left her side, and so they looked after me too. For two years after Dona died, I used to bring roses every month to the hospice ladies.

Dona was so good to me. God, she was good. She was brilliant. She was so understanding. I put her first. She put me first. We had forty-five years together. What a gift! She made me a better man. I miss her everyday. She's the one who said I should get all these stories into a book and share them with others.

Now long retired, probably what gets me through each day, besides the support of friends and calls and visits with my kids, is that I still try to help others whenever I can. It used to be volunteering, doing things for neighbors and strangers. Being less mobile now, what I can still do is give a few bucks here and there to provide a boost. I can give a smile, a kind word, an ear. I'll keep trying to do that until the end. And tell it like it is, at least for me, because honesty is the way to go and...

the truth will set you free.

DEPUTY SHERIFF · LOS ANGELES COUNTY

750

ROBERT G. MEAD
7-2-59 TO 1-3-88
RETIRED

Printed in the USA
CPSIA information can be obtained
at www.ICGtesting.com
CBHW070526230624
10483CB00009B/54

9 798988 713838